Contents

CA... NG

...s Guide

Hilary White

Card Making: A Beginner's Guide is also available in accessible formats for people with any degree of visual impairment. The large print edition and e-book (with accessibility features enabled) are available from Need2Know. Please let us know if there are any special features you require and we will do our best to accommodate your needs.

First published in Great Britain in 2013 by
Need2Know
Remus House
Coltsfoot Drive
Peterborough
PE2 9BF
Telephone 01733 898103
Fax 01733 313524
www.need2knowbooks.co.uk

SB ISBN 978-1-86144-336-6
Cover photograph: Dreamstime

Introduction

Card making is a delightful hobby that has exploded in popularity over the past few years. Whether you are a complete beginner or a confident and experienced artist, card making has something to offer just about everyone.

In line with its growing popularity, art and craft suppliers have come up with a dizzying array of resources, materials, tools and techniques. From paper punches, stamps and jewels, to textured and handmade card and paper, there is a seemingly endless supply of wonderful resources to choose from. Whatever effect you want to create, it's now possible to find the right tools to bring just about any creative idea to life.

Such choice and variety means that there has never been a better time to make your own cards. At the same time, it can be a bit confusing – and with so much to choose from, it's easy to spend a lot of money on stuff that you don't really need. It can also be tricky to work out how to use certain resources, and how to make the most of a particular tool. Although many resources are multi-use, there are some that have a specialised purpose – such as a specific type of ink pad for heat embossing or the right kind of glue for decoupage work. There are also the many different types of cards that can be made, quite apart from deciding on the design of your card and knowing where to find new ideas and inspirations.

With so much to think about, a guide to the maze of choices and possibilities is an essential – and this is what *Card Making: A Beginner's Guide* sets out to offer. Although the book is written with the beginner in mind, there are lots of tips and ideas that the more experienced crafter can make use of. It's always handy to have a guide to refer to if you want to try out a new technique or go back to a technique you haven't used for a while. Although there isn't room to explain every card-making technique in detail, the basics are covered and advice is given on how and where to find out more information.

Starting with the fundamentals of card making, chapters 1 and 2 look at card blanks, inserts and envelopes and the essential skills of cutting and sticking. Chapter 3 explores the huge variety of card, paper and sheet material available and chapters 4, 5, 6, 7 and 8 look at different techniques and embellishments – such as stamping, stickers, embossing, paper punches, ribbons, jewels, glitter and inks. Chapter 9 explores the different words and messages you can put on your cards, and chapter 10 looks at designing and selling your cards. Each chapter includes lots of tips, ideas and suggestions for using the different techniques, and advice on where to purchase tools and resources. There are numerous good sources for buying your crafting goodies – many online – and these are included in the help list at the end of the book. If an established online business is particularly good for a specific group of items, such as handmade papers, it is mentioned within the relevant chapter. The book also includes a glossary to help you make sense of crafting jargon, and a booklist so you can further explore the techniques that particularly interest you.

Whether you simply want to arrange and stick ready-cut images onto a card blank, or use creative techniques to produce a mini work of art, card making is the perfect pastime. There are few other hobbies that cater so well for just about any age group and level of expertise. If you have had some experience with card making, you will know that there is always something new for a crafter to learn. If you are new to card making, you are about to embark on an exciting and unique journey of discovery. Have fun!

Product recommendations

The products, manufacturers and websites referred to in this book are personal recommendations. Many of the mentioned brands are iconic, and they include names that you will come across time and time again as you explore the world of card making. This does not mean that these products are the only options, and there are many excellent alternatives that you can use in your card making. If you take the recommendations in this book as a starting point, you will soon find yourself building up your own personal repertoire of favourites as your crafting skills develop.

Chapter One

Card Blanks, Inserts and Envelopes

Every handmade card is unique, and there is a huge variety of techniques that you can use to decorate your card. Having said which, each card requires three basic elements:

- A card blank
- An insert
- An envelope

'Every card needs to start off with a card!'

About card blanks

Every card needs to start off with a card! In other words, a blank piece of folded cardstock that will stand up by itself and provide you with a surface to decorate.

Common shapes and sizes

Although a handmade card can be whatever size and shape you want, there are some commonly used card formats with standard measurements:

- A DL card is a tall rectangle. When folded, it measures approximately 10cm by 21cm.

- An A6 card (sometimes called C6) is the most traditional size for a greetings card. When folded, it is a quarter of an A4 sheet, measuring approximately 10.5cm by 15cm.
- Square cards typically come in small and large, with small measuring approximately 10cm by 10cm when folded and large measuring approximately 15cm by 15cm.

Card blanks can also be portrait (vertical) or landscape (horizontal) – and you can use a rectangular card with the fold to the right or the fold along the top.

Even these three basic formats give you a wide range of choices – and deciding what size, shape and orientation will work best with the design you have in mind is all part of the enjoyment. For example, a row of 'Happy Birthday' bunting can look very effective set horizontally along a long thin card. Alternatively, if you want to make a card with a tree motif, you would use the long thin card in the upright orientation.

'The card for card blanks must be sturdy enough to stand up and also take the weight of your embellishments without wrinkling.'

What card weight?

The card for card blanks must be sturdy enough to stand up and also take the weight of your embellishments without wrinkling. Card and paper is weighed in grams per square metre or gsm (see page 34 for more on paper and card weights). The weight for cardstock (as opposed to paper) ranges from around 120gsm for light card to 300gsm for heavyweight card. As a general rule, aim for card blanks that are at least 250gsm. If you have very light embellishments and are not using wet glue, you can probably get away with card as light as 220gsm. If you have heavy embellishments, you may want to go up as high as 300gsm.

Some more unusual card shapes

Apart from the basic single-fold card, there are many other ways of folding, shaping and/or cutting a card to make it a bit different . . .

Shaped cards

Shaped cards can be any shape that will stand up, including circular, triangular, egg-shaped (for Easter) heart-shaped (for Valentine's Day), numbers, cupcakes, Christmas trees, shoes – the possibilities are endless! You can buy ready-cut card blank shapes or templates to make your own. www.craftsuprint.com has a huge selection of shaped cards that you can download for less than a pound each.

Shaped edges

The edge of the card front can also be shaped with small or large scallops, deckle edges (a crinkly, torn effect), zigzags and other shapes. You can buy card blanks with shaped edges or cut your own.

Different types of fold

Folded cards range from the simple to the highly intricate. The most commonly used fold (apart from the ordinary single fold card) is the gatefold. This is a card with two fold lines so that it opens and shuts like a pair of gates. Other folds include the diamond top fold, the napkin or triangle fold, the waterfall card, the tri-fold and the easel card. There are a number of tutorials on how to fold these cards on YouTube.

A cut-away front

Cutting away half of the front of a DL card (lengthways) to reveal the inside of the card looks effective – particularly if you decorate the section that is revealed. You can also stick on a shape so that it overlaps the front.

Aperture cards

Aperture cards have a shaped hole punched into the front – usually square, rectangular, circular or oval. You can buy aperture cards or you can make your own aperture by using a craft knife to cut a straight-sided shape in the front of the card. To make apertures with curved shapes, you will need a giant paper punch – see page 23 for more on craft knives and page 79 for more on paper punches.

Using aperture cards

Aperture cards are perfect for making:

Shaker cards

Using double-sided tape, stick a piece of acetate (see chapter 3) behind the aperture. Stick foam pads all around the edge of the acetate and put a small quantity of glitter, sequins or tiny beads on the acetate. Stick a piece of patterned card, the same size as the acetate on the foam pads. Make sure there are no gaps or the glitter will fall out. There are a number of shaker card video tutorials on YouTube.

'Iris folding is a paper craft technique that involves sticking strips of paper behind an aperture to create a pattern.'

Frames

Stick patterned paper, coloured vellum or mulberry paper behind the aperture and add a special motif. Decorate around the frame on the front of the card. For more on vellum and mulberry paper, see chapter 3.

Iris folding

Iris folding is a paper craft technique that involves sticking strips of paper behind an aperture to create a pattern. It can be time-consuming, although it's not a difficult technique once you know what you're doing.

Try this – mock iris folding

- The following suggestion is not a true iris folding pattern, although it is inspired by the technique – and it's much quicker and easier.
- Choose two different papers in contrasting colours and/or patterns.
- Cut out some strips and fold the strips in half lengthways.
- Tape the strips across the back of the aperture so that they overlap, making sure that the strips are securely taped on each side.
- Set each strip at a slight angle, some tilting one way and some the other – and don't worry if the strips are slightly different widths as this adds to the overall effect.
- When the entire aperture has been covered, you will see a textured, striped pattern from the front.

If you want to find out more about true iris folding, see the book list. There are also some useful tutorials on YouTube.

Buying and making card blanks

You can either buy ready-made card blanks, or you can make your own:

Buying card blanks

Card blanks are available from craft shops and craft websites. You can buy them in packs or you can order the number, colour and size you want online. www.pdacardandcraft.co.uk offers good value for money and has a varied selection. You can pick out exactly the size and shape of card blank you want, order it in a wide range of different colours, finishes and textures – and also order any quantity. If you prefer not to order online, most web-based companies will also accept phone or mail orders.

Making card blanks

As an alternative to buying card blanks, you can cut and fold your own. You will need to cut out twice the width of the card front so that you can fold it – for example, a folded card measuring 15cm by 15cm requires a piece of card measuring 30cm by 15cm.

A scoring board and a bone folder are useful tools if you want to make your own card blanks:

- A scoring board is a board with a series of deep grooves. Most scoring boards are marked with measurements, and some indicate where to measure and score if you want to make different sized cards. There are several branded scoring boards, including the Hougie, Scor-Pal and Eazi-Score boards. They have many other uses, apart from folding simple card blanks – and crafters tend to be loyal to different brands. If you want to invest in a scoring board, it's worth doing an Internet search for reviews of the different boards before deciding which one is best for you.
- A bone folder is a flattish, blunt-edged tool, rounded at one end and pointed at the other. Many bone folders are actually made from bone, although you can also get plastic or wooden ones. Even if you don't have a scoring board, a bone folder is useful as you can run it firmly along your fold to give it a crisp finish.

'Card makers never throw anything away; keep a box for scraps of card and paper.'

To fold a card using a scoring board, simply place the centre of the card over a groove in the scoring board and run the bone folder along the groove. This creates a deep score in the card, making it much easier to fold and giving the fold a neat, clean edge. You can also use a ball-tipped embossing tool to score with – some card makers find this works better than a bone folder. For more on embossing tools, see chapter 6.

When you cut out card to fold into card blanks, you will have lots of offcuts. Card makers never throw anything away; keep a box for scraps of card and paper and use them for small printed images, making labels, punching out shapes, mounting sentiments – the list of possible uses is endless!

Which colour card blank?

The basic colours to start off with are white, and either cream or ivory. Ivory is halfway between white and cream – warmer in colour than white but not quite such a rich colour as cream.

As a general rule, aim to use a white card blank with cold colours (blues, silvers, violets, greys, black) and ivory or cream with warm colours (yellows, oranges, greens, browns, golds). However, rules are there to be broken – particularly in card making. Look at the colours you are working with and hold them against the card blank before deciding. Sometimes gold on white or pale blue on cream look fabulous.

Apart from the basic white, ivory and cream, you can use any colour you want for your card blank. Pastel pinks and pale greens are lovely for Easter and Mother's Day cards; red, dark green or silver work well for Christmas cards, and bold primary colours are good for children's cards. You can also use card blanks with a textured finish, such as pearlescent, embossed, glittered or hammered. Choosing the colour, finish and texture of your card blank is all part of your overall design.

For more on the many different types of card textures and finishes available, see chapter 3.

Inserts

An insert is a lovely way to finish off your cards.

What is an insert?

An insert is a piece of folded paper that is attached to the inside of the card. You don't have to make an insert, but it gives your handmade card a much better finish – and it's also easier to write a message on an insert, rather than the inside of the card itself.

Making inserts

Inserts are not difficult to make. Simply cut out a rectangle of paper, measuring the length and width of the rectangle about a centimetre smaller than the card. Fold the rectangle in half and attach to the inside of the card. If you make the insert the same size as the card, it tends to poke out when the card is closed.

There are various ways of attaching your insert. Put a strip of thin double-sided tape or dots of PVA glue down the inside fold of the card and attach the insert. Some card makers also put a little adhesive behind the insert, to the left and the right of the fold, so that the insert opens with the card. You can also stick the insert to the inner left or right-hand side of the card, instead of down the fold. Try out different techniques and use the one that works best for you.

Colour and decoration

The insert can be any colour, although your written message shows up better on white, cream, ivory or a pastel colour. You can also use any paper finish, as long as it can be written on; pearlescent or vellum papers are popular for inserts (for more on different papers, see chapter 3).

Choosing an insert colour that picks up the colour of the embellishments on the card can look very effective. For example, a baby boy card might be decorated with pale blue gingham ribbon on a cream card. A pale blue insert will co-ordinate with the colour of the ribbon and look pretty against the cream.

As with the card, the insert can be decorated with stamped images, stencils, sprays and chalks. You can also punch shapes along the edges and into the corners of the insert.

Messages

Printing messages and verses on the insert is another option. If you don't want to have a go at making up your own verses, there are lots of free verses on the Internet – although they do vary in quality. Many crafting CDs have a sentiments and verses section that you can print directly onto your insert (for more on crafting CDs, see chapter 3). If you want a book of words to choose from, try *Just the Right Words: Over 400 Messages and Motifs for Cardmakers and Crafters* (see the book list for details).

Buying inserts

If you make lots of cards and tend to use the same size card blank, buying ready-cut inserts saves time. You can buy packs of inserts, or order the size, colour and paper type you want from websites such as www.pdacardandcraft.co.uk. This company will also print your inserts with specific sentiments, such as 'Happy Birthday' or 'Congratulations on the birth of your child'.

Envelopes

Every card must have an envelope – and as with all aspects of card making, there are lots of creative options . . .

'For the card-maker, a plain envelope is an opportunity for yet more crafting and creativity.'

Buying envelopes

If you order card blanks online, you can also order envelopes that match in both size and colour. Sites such as www.pdacardandcraft.co.uk tell you which envelopes fit the card size you are ordering. If you buy packs of ready-made card blanks, they should come with matching envelopes.

Decorating envelopes

For the card maker, a plain envelope is an opportunity for yet more crafting and creativity. Any decorative techniques can be used to jazz up your envelope – and decorating the envelope to match the card makes it all the more special. Stamping and colouring images, embossing, stencilling, using chalks and sprays are all good choices for decorating an envelope. See chapter 4 for everything you need to know about stamping and chapter 6 for embossing and stencilling.

If your envelope flap has a straight edge, you can use a border punch to punch a pattern along the edge of the flap. Stick a strip of coloured paper behind the punched out shapes and seal the envelope with a dab of glue or a clear round sticker. If your envelope has a triangular flap, punch a small shape into the point at the tip of the flap and back it with coloured paper. See chapter 5 for more about using punches.

Sticking on pictures or embellishments is yet another option, although you need to make sure that everything is flat and well stuck if you are planning to post your card.

Lining envelopes

A lined envelope looks special – and you can choose a lining paper to match or complement your card. The technique is quite simple if you follow these steps:

1. Open up the flap of your envelope.
2. Measure the length of the envelope, from the tip of the flap to the bottom.
3. Measure the width of the envelope.
4. Subtract about 3mm from the width and about 1.3cm from the length (if you prefer working in inches, this equates to approximately 1/8" and ½").
5. Using these measurements cut out a rectangle from scrap card, such as cereal box card.
6. Check that the rectangle slides comfortably into your envelope and that its upper edge sits below the line of glue at the tip of the flap.
7. Take out the card, place it on the table and place the envelope on top.
8. Line up the envelope centrally with the card, making sure that the tip of the envelope is touching the top of the card.
9. Trace the two diagonal lines of the flap onto the card and cut them out.
10. Check that the template slides into the envelope and does not cover the adhesive on the flap.
11. Draw round the template on your lining paper and cut out the shape to

make a liner. If you place the template against the edge and bottom of the paper, it minimises the cutting. Use a paper cutter or craft knife to get straight lines.

12. Slide the liner into the envelope, fold over the envelope flap to crease the liner and glue the upper part of the liner to the flap (use a dryish glue such as a glue stick, or double sided tape – see chapter 2 for information about different types of adhesive).

Whenever you make a card template, save it so that you can reuse it for envelopes of the same size and shape.

Making envelopes

For a truly unique look, make a special envelope from scratch. The easiest way to do this is to open up an envelope in the size you want and turn it into a template. Draw round the template on patterned paper, cut out the envelope shape, mark the lines in pencil, fold along the lines and glue the envelope together. You can also download free envelope templates from the Internet (try www.allcrafts.net).

If you use a colourful patterned paper for your envelope, you will need to stick on a plain label for the name and address. You can also make a decorative label by punching patterns into a paper shape and sticking it on the front of the envelope.

Stick down the flap of your envelope using double-sided tape. It is also possible to buy Lick and Stick envelope glue. Paint it onto the flap of your homemade envelope, leave to dry and it will be ready for you to lick and stick whenever you want to use the envelope. Alternatively, you can make a feature of sealing the envelope by using a pretty circular sticker.

Making box envelopes

A box envelope is a cross between a box and an envelope (some crafters refer to them as 'boxelopes'). A box envelope is required if your handmade card has lots of embellishments and is too thick to go into a regular envelope. A box envelope is also useful if your card is delicate and needs the protection of a box.

There are several tutorials on YouTube, showing you how to make a box envelope. Some of the demonstrations use a branded, multi-purpose scoring board, such as the Hougie. If you want to make envelopes, boxelopes or boxes on a regular basis, it's well worth investing in a scoring board.

Summing Up

- As a starting point, every handmade card needs a card blank, an insert and an envelope.
- Card blanks can be bought ready-made, or you can make them yourself. A scoring board and bone folder are useful tools if you want to make your own card blanks.
- Card blanks come in all shapes and sizes, and they can be whatever texture or colour you choose – as long as the card is sturdy enough to stand up and take the weight of your embellishments.
- An insert is not essential, but it gives your card a professional finish – and it's much easier to write a message on an insert than the inside of the card itself.
- Envelopes can be bought ready-made, or you can make them yourself using a template.
- Envelopes can be made from patterned paper or decorated with a variety of techniques to complement the card.

Chapter Two

Cutting and Sticking

Cutting and sticking are the two basic, practical skills required to make your own handmade cards. Don't worry if you haven't done much cutting or sticking since primary school; there are lots of different products to help you achieve the effect you are looking for – and there are also techniques to match every level of skill.

Cutting tools and techniques

If you are handy with a pair of scissors, you can go ahead and cut out complex shapes and motifs for your cards. If, however, the thought of using scissors throws you into a panic, or you have difficulties with dexterity, there are many other cutting tools to choose from.

'As with many crafting tools, it's worth paying extra for good-quality scissors.'

Scissors – the basics

Scissors are the first cutting tool that we tend to think of – and even if you don't plan to do much cutting out with scissors, you will still need a good pair for cutting materials such as ribbon and tape.

It's useful to have at least two pairs of scissors in different sizes – a small pair for fine work and a larger pair for when you want to cut a larger piece of paper or card. As with many crafting tools, it's worth paying extra for good-quality scissors. Fiskars (the ones with orange handles), X-Cut and Tonic are all well-respected names in the crafting world.

Keeping your scissors sharp is essential. You can invest in a scissor sharpener – or try cutting through aluminium foil or medium grade sandpaper. Some crafters keep separate scissors for fabric and paper, as fabric tends to blunt scissors more quickly than paper.

Scissors for the left-handed

Cutting is notoriously difficult for many left-handed people. If you are left-handed and struggle with cutting, try using specially designed scissors. Left-handed scissors have the blades and finger holes reversed, making them more comfortable to hold and enabling you to see what you are doing.

Another option is big loop scissors. Small scissors usually have small handles, but Fiskars make a pair that combine small, thin blades with large looped handles. The loops are suitable for both left and right-handed crafters, and they are also good if you have arthritis.

See the help list for online stores selling left-handed scissors and scissors for crafters with dexterity difficulties.

Fancy scissors

Apart from ordinary, straight-bladed scissors, you can also buy fancy scissors for cutting a shaped edge. Deckle, scalloped, postage stamp and wavy edged blades are just a few of the available choices – and pinking shears are also great for cutting zigzag lines. If you are not confident about cutting a straight line with ordinary scissors, good-quality pinking shears will hide a wobbly edge – as well as producing a more interesting effect.

Decoupage scissors

Decoupage scissors have small, narrow, pointed blades, enabling crafters to cut out intricate shapes with precision (see chapter 7 for more on decoupage). Decoupage scissors often have tweezer-like handles (they are sometimes called decoupage snips). The squeezing action places less pressure on the fingers than finger holes, which can be useful for crafters with dexterity difficulties. Some crafters swear by the tweezer handle whereas others find them harder to manipulate than the traditional scissor handle.

Cutting out with scissors – some practical tips

- Always choose the right scissors for the job.
- Keep your scissors sharp.
- When cutting out complex shapes, move the paper rather than the scissors.
- Cut out shapes from the edge of the paper rather than the centre. This avoids wasting paper.
- When cutting out a shape, cut roughly around it first. It's much easier to cut from a small rather than a large piece of paper.
- Cut near the angle of the scissor blades, rather than the tips.
- Cut slowly, and aim for long cuts rather than quick snips. If parts of a shape are intricate or angled, go back to them later and cut them out using the tips of your scissors.
- Scissors are not always the best tool for the job. Choose other cutting implements where necessary – see following.

'When cutting out complex shapes, move the paper rather than the scissors.'

Craft knives

A craft knife is a sharp single blade set into a plastic or metal handle. You can buy packs of disposable knives, or change the blade of your knife as it becomes blunt. Craft knives are seriously sharp. Keep well away from children and pets, and store the knife with its cover on. Although a little more expensive, you can also buy craft knives with retractable blades.

A craft knife is a quick and easy way of cutting an absolutely straight edge. Simply place your paper or card on a board or cutting mat, place a metal ruler on the paper, hold the ruler firm and draw your blade along the ruler's edge to slice through the paper. The ruler must be metal rather than plastic or wood – the blade of a craft knife is so sharp that it will slice chunks out of anything that isn't metal.

The sharp tip of a craft knife is also useful for cutting around intricate shapes, although it's worth practising this technique before trying to cut out something special.

Rotary paper trimmers

Rotary paper trimmers are good for cutting straight edges. A rotary paper trimmer has a wheel-shaped blade set into a movable shuttle and mounted on a sturdy pole and base. The base usually has a grid and measurements, to help you cut the size of paper that you want. It's almost impossible to cut yourself with a paper trimmer (unlike a craft knife or scissors). When the wheel blade gets blunt, it can be replaced – so it's worth buying a well-known make and ensuring that you can get a steady supply of replacement blades.

Some rotary trimmers include fancy blades, enabling you to cut scalloped, deckle, zigzag, wavy or serrated edges. They also come in a range of different sizes. There are a huge number of paper trimmers on the market and crafters tend to have their favourites. Before making a purchase, do an Internet search for reviews of the different trimmers, to help you decide which is the right one for you. Also bear in mind that you get what you pay for – and a paper trimmer is such a key piece of equipment, it's worth spending as much as you can afford.

Read the instructions carefully before using; don't attempt to cut a heavier or thicker piece of card than recommended, as it can dislodge the rotary blade.

Guillotines

Guillotines have a different design from paper cutters. The guillotine consists of a curved blade attached to the edge of the cutter base, and the blade is pulled downwards to cut the paper. The guillotine is much less safe than the paper trimmer and should be kept well away from children. It can also be trickier to use than the rotary trimmer, as the paper or card sometimes shifts when the blade is pulled down.

The advantage of the guillotine is its capacity to cut thicker materials than the paper trimmer. It is also easy to see exactly where on the paper the blade will cut – not always the case with some paper trimmers. A good-quality guillotine tends to be more expensive than a good-quality paper trimmer.

Circle cutters, paper punches and die cutters

It's very difficult to cut out a circle with scissors. Fortunately, there are several crafting tools that will cut circles and other curved shapes. The Fiskars Ultra-Shape Xpress Shape Cutter can be used to cut freehand curved shapes, or a range of shapes using their specially designed templates.

Paper punches and die cutting machines are another option for cutting out curved shapes, without having to use scissors. For more about paper punches and die cutting machines, see chapter 5.

Tearing

As an alternative to the cut edge, tearing paper is a popular technique for card making. It creates an organic, natural look, and works particularly well with lightweight handmade papers.

To create a controlled tear, place a ruler on the paper and tear along its edge. If you want to explore torn edges further, it's worth investing in tearing rulers. These rulers have a shaped edge, such as a deckle. When you tear along them, the shaped edge of the ruler gives a more interesting torn effect than a regular ruler.

For more on tearing handmade papers, see page 44.

'As an alternative to the cut edge, tearing paper is a popular technique for card making.'

Sticking – different types of adhesive

As with cutting tools, there are lots of different adhesives to choose from. Each one does a different job – and it's useful to know what is available so that you can stick your paper, card and embellishments as neatly and securely as possible.

Adhesives for card making fall into two broad categories: wet adhesives and dry adhesives.

Wet adhesives

Wet adhesives can be spread onto any shape, and they also come in different strengths and thicknesses:

PVA craft glue

White PVA craft glue is useful for certain tasks, although it doesn't count as an all-purpose glue when it comes to card making. PVA tends to soak into card and paper, warping them and creating wrinkles once it has dried. Its main use is for sticking handmade or tissue paper shapes that are too delicate to hold either a stronger glue or a dry adhesive.

Regular PVA isn't strong enough to stick anything heavier than a paper or lightweight card embellishment. It's also not very good for sticking smooth, non-porous surfaces such as acetate.

Try this – sticking mulberry paper shapes

To stick a delicate mulberry tissue paper shape, use a spatula (or your finger) to spread PVA glue over the shape. Make sure that every part of the shape is covered in as thin a layer as possible and place it carefully on your background. Put a sheet of copier paper over the shape and rub your hand across to make sure that every part is pressed down. Finish off by putting the glued shape between two pieces of kitchen towel and placing it under a heavy book so that it dries flat. Check from time to time to make sure the glued shape is not sticking to the paper towels.

Tacky glue

Tacky glue is an extra strong, thick version of PVA glue. It usually comes in a gold bottle with a nozzle. Unlike regular PVA, it's great for sticking heavy 3D items such as charms, buttons and flat-backed jewels. It dries clear, and it also retains its flexibility when dry.

If you want to stick tiny items such as flat-backed gems, use a cocktail stick or pokey tool to apply spots of glue, either to the item itself or the card background.

> **Pokey tools**
>
> A pokey tool is a must-have craft item with a hundred-and-one uses. It consists of a sharp metal point set into a plastic or metal handle – and once you get one, you'll wonder how you ever managed without it!

Silicone glue

Silicone glue is a clear adhesive with a strong hold. Unlike tacky PVA, it retains its shape once dry – which makes it a good choice for sticking on layers to create a 3D effect (see decoupage in chapter 7). Like tacky PVA, it stays flexible when dry and works well for sticking heavy 3D embellishments. Tacky PVA sometimes soaks into a light card or paper and causes wrinkles – particularly if you need to use a good blob. Silicone glue makes a useful alternative for sticking 3D embellishments onto delicate paper such as vellum. It can also be used on card, metal, plastic, glass, ceramic and wood.

'A pokey tool is a must-have craft item with a hundred-and-one uses.'

Unlike the PVAs, silicone glue is not suitable for children. It has rather a strong smell and can be irritating to the skin. Make sure you buy a silicone glue designed for craft use, rather than DIY. If you want the advantages of silicone glue without the silicone, try the odourless and silicone-free Pinflair Glue Gel.

Spray adhesives

Spray adhesives can be expensive – but they are sometimes the best tool for a particular job. Spray adhesives are great for covering an area with a very fine and even layer of glue – just what you need when you want to stick an intricate cut-out shape, such as a lace doily. There are many different types of spray adhesive, including repositionable spray, mounting spray and photograph spray. Most spray adhesives remain tacky for a short while – which gives you a few moments to lift off your paper and reposition it before the glue dries.

On the minus side, spray adhesives are messy to use and they smell quite strong. You also need to do some research before buying. Some don't stick very well, so check out customer reviews online before deciding which brand to go for. Make sure also that you are buying a spray adhesive for paper craft and not DIY.

Applying a spray adhesive

Mist the adhesive across the card or paper to create a fine, even layer. If you spray the adhesive directly at the paper, you can end up with pools of glue. Use spray adhesives in a well-ventilated room – or even outside if the weather allows.

Glue pens

'Glue pens are useful for precision gluing.'

As its name suggests, a glue pen is similar to an ordinary pen except that it is filled with glue rather than ink. Glue pens are useful for precision gluing – although the main reason to keep a glue pen in your collection is for glitter and heat embossing. A good-quality glue pen writes just like a gel pen; this enables you to draw shapes and write messages which can then be sprinkled with glitter or heat embossed. The Sakura Quickie Glue pen is one of the best on the market. It goes on blue so you can see what you are doing – but dries clear, like PVA glue.

Glue sticks

Glue sticks are quick and easy to use, and they are useful for card making with children. The main disadvantage (and it's a big disadvantage!) is their lack of permanence. Paper and other items stuck on with a glue stick tend to drop off after a while – not ideal for a handmade card, particularly if you are selling your creations.

Dry adhesives

Dry adhesives are not as malleable as wet adhesives, but they have the huge advantage of not wrinkling paper:

Double-sided adhesive tape

Double-sided tape comes in a roll. Both sides of the tape are sticky, with one side covered in protective paper. To use it, you simply peel a strip of tape from the roll, stick it to your background, peel off the protective paper to reveal the second sticky side and place your card or paper on top. It's perfect for sticking two pieces of card or paper together without causing wrinkles – although once stuck down, it's permanent and very secure.

Double-sided tape comes in different widths and strengths. For super strong tape, look out for the red rolls (the tape itself is clear, but the lining paper is red). Most red double-sided tape is heat resistant as well as extra sticky, making it suitable to use for heat embossing (see chapter 6). You can also get tape with a margin of protective paper overlapping the edge of the tape – called finger lift tape. It's much easier to peel off the paper, but harder to position the tape right at the edge of the card, as you can't see where the sticky bit begins and ends.

Double-sided adhesive sheets

Double-sided adhesive sheets are similar to double-sided tape, except they come in sheet form. The sheets can be cut to shape, punched or die cut (see chapter 5). Double-sided adhesive sheets are also an essential if you want to use gilding flakes or make lacy glitter patterns (see chapter 8).

Adhesive dots

Adhesive dots are tiny spots of dry adhesive that usually come on a roll of tape. They are also known as sticky dots or glue dots. To use, you simply press the tape against the card or paper so that the dots transfer to the surface of the card. Adhesive dots are handy for sticking an item with an irregular shape. They are also quick and easy to use, but they can work out quite expensive if you want to stick large areas. Some brands also work better than others – so do your research before deciding which brand to buy.

Tape runners

Tape runners or rollers are plastic dispensers containing double-sided tape. To use the tape runner, roll it along your card or paper to leave a strip of adhesive. Tape runners are quick, easy and satisfying to use. As long as they are good quality, they stick extremely well and you can also position the adhesive exactly where you want it.

On the downside, many tape runners are disposable so they can be quite an expensive option. They are also not the best choice if you are concerned about the environmental impact of your crafting. It is possible to buy refillable tape runners, although they are initially more expensive than the disposable type.

Sticky tape

'If you want an element of your card to be raised, foam pads are a quick and easy adhesive to use.'

Clear sticky tape is not often used for card making as it is a rather visible form of adhesive. Regular clear tape also tends to turn yellow and peel off after a while. It is possible to buy clear sticky tape circles, which are useful for sealing envelopes. They also make a neat way of securing certain embellishments, such as the ends of a ribbon hidden behind another embellishment or insert.

Foam pads and foam tape

Like double-sided tape, foam pads are sticky on both sides. If you want an element of your card to be raised, foam pads are a quick and easy adhesive to use. Along with silicone glue, foam pads are the main adhesive choice for giving dimension to decoupage work (see chapter 7).

Foam pads come in various sizes and thicknesses, and you can cut them into smaller pieces if necessary. Although the majority of foam pads are white, you can get them in black for dark embellishments. You can also colour the foam with felt pens to match the colour of an embellishment.

Foam tape is similar to foam pads except that it comes in tape form, enabling you to cut off the quantity you need.

Sticker machines

If you have plenty of cash to invest in crafting, a sticker machine is worth considering. Sticker machines work by covering the back of a shape with an even layer of adhesive. This is by far the quickest, neatest and easiest way of sticking an intricate flat shape. If you decide to go for a sticker machine, Xyron is a well-known company – and it's always worth going for an established manufacturer when you buy something that needs refills.

> **Scissors for adhesive tape**
>
> Cutting double-sided tape and foam tape makes a mess of your scissors. Most crafters keep a special pair of scissors just for this job, and you can also buy Teflon-coated scissors to prevent the blades from getting gummed up.
>
> When you need to clean your gluey scissors, try rubbing them with tea tree essential oil, eucalyptus oil or nail polish remover.

Summing Up

- Cutting and sticking are the two basic skills required for making cards.
- There is a huge variety of cutting tools to choose from, ranging from scissors to die cutting machines.
- If you are not confident with scissors, there are lots of other cutting options – although practice makes perfect and your scissor skills will improve the more you use them.
- Adhesives fall into two categories: wet (such as tacky PVA glue, silicone glue and glue pens) and dry (such as double-sided tape, glue dots and foam pads).
- Choosing the right glue for a particular task is important in ensuring that your card looks neat – and everything stays firmly stuck!

Chapter Three

Paper, Card and Sheet Material

If cutting and sticking are the basic, practical skills needed for card making, paper and card are the basic materials. There is a huge variety of different colours, patterns, textures and finishes to choose from – and every card maker has their own particular favourites

In this chapter, we look at what is available, ways of using different types of paper and card, where to buy from and sheet materials that do not fall into the paper or card category.

Paper and card sizes

When you buy paper or card, it will usually come in standard sizes:

- A4: printer paper size – 297mm x 210mm
- A5: half A4 size – 210mm x 148mm
- A3: double A4 size – 420mm x 297mm
- A2: double A3 size – 594mm x 420mm
- Standard size square scrapbooking paper – 12" x 12" (30cm x 30cm)
- Small square scrapbooking paper – 6" x 6" (15cm x 15cm)

A4

This is the most common size for paper and card (the size of copier paper, for example). If you want to make your own card blanks, you will need cardstock to be at least A4 size.

A5

A few suppliers offer paper and card in this size, and some paper packs come in A5. If you want to use a particular paper for making small shapes and embellishments, A5 is both cheaper and easier to work with than larger sheets.

'If you want to use a particular paper for making small shapes and embellishments, A5 is both cheaper and easier to work with than larger sheets.'

A3 and A2

A few suppliers offer paper and card in these large sizes. It is more unwieldy to work with than A4 or A5 – but necessary if you want to make your own larger card blanks.

Square scrapbooking paper

Patterned scrapbooking paper is designed to fit into standard-sized scrapbooks. It is measured in inches because it is an American product. For more about scrapbooking paper, see page 45.

Paper and card weights

Paper is weighed as grams per square metre (gsm). When you buy paper or card, the gsm number will tell you how sturdy it is.

The lower the gsm number, the thinner and lighter the paper or card. There isn't a clear cut-off point between paper and card, although paper from 120gsm upwards is often referred to as card. Specialist paper manufacturers regard it all as paper, calling heavier paper cardstock paper.

From the card maker's point of view, the weight of the paper/card is what matters. You need to have a minimum weight of card to make card blanks – and you mustn't use paper above a certain weight and thickness in paper punches and rotary trimmers.

The rough guide to paper and card weights is as follows:

- Copy paper (used in printers) is around 70 to 80gsm.
- Tissue paper can be anything between 10 and 35gsm.
- Lightweight card starts at around 120gsm.
- Card for making card blanks needs to be at least 250gsm, and heavier if possible.
- Board is generally thicker than cardstock, and measured in microns rather than gsm; for example, 1,000 micron = 1mm thickness. It is made from pulp and coated to give it a smooth surface and colour.

You should be able to use up to 120gsm in your computer printer. Many printers will take a heavier cardstock – but always check the manufacturer's recommendations.

Paper and card – the different types

In this section, we run through the different finishes, textures and types of paper and card. As you will see, there is a huge range to choose from.

Online card and paper stores

If you are buying online, www.craftcreations.com offer one of the widest choices of paper and card in the UK. They also do small sample packs, enabling you to try out a paper before deciding to buy in larger quantities. pdacardandcraft.co.uk is another excellent source. They provide cheap sample swatches so you can check what a paper looks like in 'real life'.

Hammer, linen and laid finishes

Card and paper come in various finishes – and hammer, linen and laid are three of the most common:

- Hammer paper and card have a bumpy, stippled effect – as if they have been hammered.
- Linen paper and card have a subtle, woven texture similar to that of fine linen.

- Laid paper and card have a texture made up of fine ridges.

Hammer, linen and laid paper and card usually come in white, ivory or cream. Cardstock with a texture makes a more interesting card blank, and also works well as a surface for printing sentiments (see chapter 9).

Copier and printing paper

Ordinary copier paper has some uses in card making, such as inserts for your cards – although you will mostly want to use paper with a higher quality surface or finish. You can buy copier paper in different colours, which work particularly well for inserts.

If you want to print out images from a craft CD, look out for super smooth paper or card (sometimes called super smooth decoupage paper). This will give an added brightness and clarity to your printing. Super smooth paper also works well for stamping projects (see chapter 4).

Core'dinations paper

Core'dinations is a beautiful, heavyweight paper that has a different coloured core from the outer surfaces of the paper. For example, the surface may be chocolate with a turquoise core, or black with a purple core. One side of the paper is textured and the other side is smooth.

There are lots of different effects you can achieve with Core'dinations paper:

Tearing

Tearing Core'dinations paper produces an interesting edge as you get the coloured core showing through.

Distressing

Use a distressing tool (see text box on the following page) to distress the edges of the paper, creating a rough edge with a different quality from a torn edge. You can also experiment with a bone folder, a craft knife (taking care it doesn't slip) or even your fingernails.

Sanding

Gently sand the textured side with sandpaper (or better still, a hand-held Tim Holtz Idea-ology sanding block). This produces a shadowy woven pattern as the sandpaper erodes the raised lines to reveal the contrasting core colour underneath.

Crumpling

Crumple up a shape cut from Core'dinations paper, smooth it out and then sand over the wrinkles.

Shape rubbing

Try placing a raised shape (such as a wooden letter) under the paper and rubbing over with a sanding block. This is a similar technique to wax rubbing, except that you are using sandpaper rather than a wax crayon.

> **Distressed papercrafting**
>
> The distressed or grungy style of crafting has been pioneered by American designer Tim Holtz. He sells a range of distressing tools specially designed to rough up the edges of thick paper or card. For more information, visit Tim's website at www.timholtz.com.

'Pearlescent card and paper add a luxurious touch to wedding invitations.'

Pearlescent card and paper

Pearlescent card and paper has a beautiful, soft pearly finish. Although it comes in all colours, it's particularly effective in pastel shades such as pale pink, lemon and baby blue.

Pearlescent card works particularly well for dry embossing (see chapter 6), as the pearly finish throws the embossed pattern into relief. You can also buy pearlescent card that is ready embossed with simple motifs such as dots, stars or lattice patterns.

White, ivory, cream, silver, baby blue and pink pearlescent card and paper add a luxurious touch to wedding invitations, christening or new baby cards. Try making pearlescent paper inserts and envelopes for handmade wedding invitations. You should be able to print on the paper with your regular printer, although some printers work better than others. Experiment first – and if you intend to do a lot of printing on pearlescent (perhaps you are planning to start a handmade wedding stationery business) carry out an online search for crafters' recommendations.

Glitter card and paper

Glitter card or paper is useful for adding sparkly accents such as a glittered strip down the edge of the card, a glittery shape or a glittery background. It ranges from thickly glittered paper to a subtle glitter that is embedded in the card itself. Some glitter card is coloured card with a clear or pearlescent glitter on top.

Glitter card is easier to handle than loose glitter, and it doesn't shed in the same way – particularly if you buy the type that is fused into the surface of the card. On the flip side, it isn't as versatile as loose glitter and you can't use it to create effects such as glittering a transparent outline peel-off (see chapter 5). Be wary about cutting heavily glittered paper or card with your rotary trimmer and paper punches. A sturdy punch may cope with lightweight glitter card – but it's safer to use scissors rather than your trimmer if you want a straight edge. Use a pencil and ruler to make a guideline on the un-glittered back of the card. Take slow, careful cuts with a large pair of scissors – and remember that the glitter itself should hide a slightly wobbly edge!

Mirri card and paper

Mirri usually comes as card, although www.craftcreations.com also sells it as paper. The term 'mirri' is short for mirror – and you really can see your face in this fabulously shiny card. Gold and silver are the most common colours, although you can get it in all colours. Black mirri is a particularly effective and useful finish if you like making cards with a black and white colour theme. Mirri is also available with a silk finish. Silk mirri is less shiny than regular mirri and has a silky shimmer.

Gold and silver mirri card is perfect for Christmas or Diwali cards – and for adding a contrasting texture to matting and layering (see chapter 10 for more on matting and layering).

Corrugated card

Corrugated card is fluted to create a unique texture. It usually comes in a natural, cardboard colour, although it is also available in a range of other colours. Micro-corrugated card has narrower flutes – which work better for smaller details.

Corrugated card makes an interesting mount for a picture embellishment, although it looks more effective if the flutes are horizontal rather than vertical.

A thin strip towards the edge or across the top of a card also looks good.

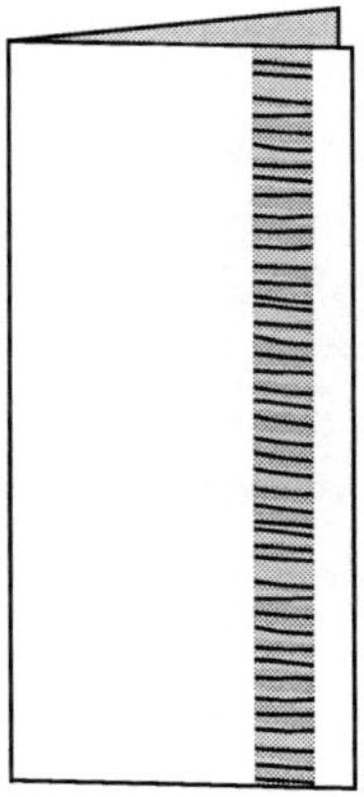

Corrugated card is also useful for details that require a fluted texture – such as the roof of a house for a 'Good Luck in Your New Home' card, or the body of a boat for a man's birthday card. Try punching shapes from micro-fluted corrugated card with a sturdy paper punch or die cutting machine.

Try this – a corrugated embellishment

A simple shape cut from coloured corrugated card and decorated with ribbon, winding thread or buttons looks very effective mounted on a square of natural coloured corrugated card. Make sure that the flutes go one way on the background square and the other way on the shape.

Try this – a corrugated boat

To make a textured boat for a man's card, cut out a simple boat shape from corrugated card and add punched circles to represent portholes. Cut two triangular sails from card and mount them on cocktail stick masts. Cut out a flag to stick to the top of the sails, with a birthday sentiment.

Grungeboard and chipboard

Although grungeboard and chipboard have some similarities, they are quite different products:

Grungeboard

Grungeboard was developed by Tim Holtz (see the book list and help list). Made from compressed paper fibres, it's a pliable, leathery material that is suitable for all types of decoration. It comes in sheets, or you can buy it ready cut in a variety of different shapes (called Grungeboard Elements). Grungeboard is a textured material, with a stronger texture on one side and a lighter texture on the other.

Grungeboard is unusually tough. It's virtually impossible to tear, and you can bend or twist it without cracking the fibres (think leather, rather than card). This makes it a useful product for creating flowers with curled petals, or butterflies with curved wings, or bendable hinges for a book. Grungeboard can take any amount of inking, spraying, enamelling and heating without losing its shape or getting soggy. It can also be sewn and is tough enough to be used for making key rings or bangles. Perhaps the one disadvantage of Grungeboard is its strong, chemically smell. This can be a problem if you have a sensitive nose, as the smell never fully goes away.

You can also get Grungepaper, a thinner version of Grungeboard.Grungeboard is too thick for some die cutting machines. Grungepaper is a safer bet if you want to die cut or punch your own shapes, rather than buy them ready cut.

Chipboard

Although it has the same name, crafting chipboard is quite different from the DIY woodchip product. Crafting chipboard is a stiff board made from recycled paper. Like Grungeboard, you can use it for inking, spraying and heat embossing. Unlike Grungeboard, it can be torn and it also cracks when bent. Chipboard is a porous material so inks soak in, resulting in a different look from inked Grungeboard. Overall, it is not as tough or as versatile as Grungeboard. It does, however, have a smoother surface – and is completely odour free!

Check that your die cutting machine will take the thickness of chipboard if you want to cut out your own shapes. A large paper punch may be able cut through thin chipboard – but as a rule, chipboard is not suitable for punches.

'Grungeboard can take any amount of inking, spraying, enamelling and heating without losing its shape or getting soggy.'

Vellum

In the world of card making, vellum is not a traditional parchment made from calf skin but a thin, translucent paper that is similar in appearance and texture to tracing paper. Vellum comes in many different colours – and you can also buy marbled, pearlescent, foiled, glittered and embossed vellum.

Using vellum

Vellum makes a beautiful surface for dry embossing. You can also heat emboss, stamp images, use vellum as a background for outline stickers and punch shapes from vellum. For more on these techniques and the particular challenges of using them with vellum, see chapters 4, 5 and 6.

Because of its translucence, vellum can be fixed over a strongly coloured image. The vellum softens the image, giving it a romantic look – and using vellum with a misty white embossed pattern adds to the effect.

Cutting and tearing vellum

'Card makers come up with many imaginative ways of adhering vellum to their cards – and often create a beautiful effect in the process!'

Vellum is a crisp paper that both cuts and tears easily. A torn strip fixed across a card, or a torn square used as a background looks effective. For added visual interest, try inking the torn edges with an ink pad. Vellum also looks good cut with fancy scissors to create a scalloped or deckled edge, or punched with a border punch and set over dark paper (see chapter 5 for more on border punches).

Vellum for sentiments

Many card makers use vellum for adding sentiments to cards. An effective technique is to print a sentiment onto vellum, tear or cut around the sentiment to create a strip and fix the strip to the card with brads (for details on how to use brads, see chapter 7). Most inkjet printers will print onto vellum – although it may take quite a while for the ink to dry as the surface of the vellum is so smooth. If you find that your words are smudging, try minimising the ink by printing on a draft setting – and make sure that that none of the words are in bold. Make sure also that the vellum isn't curled at the corners, or you may have problems with paper feed.

Sticking vellum

Although vellum is a lovely paper to work with, it's tricky to attach to a card because both wet and dry adhesives tend to show through. For this reason, card makers come up with many imaginative ways of adhering vellum to their cards – and often create a beautiful effect in the process!

Try the following:

- Use brads to attach a vellum shape – at the top and bottom for a shape such as an oval, on the four corners for a rectangle or at each end of a strip (see chapter 7 for more on brads).
- Attach your vellum with an adhesive and cover with an embellishment, such as a button, a flower or a bow. For example, a torn strip of vellum could have a brad at one end and be glued at the other, with a flower motif to hide where the adhesive shows through.
- Stitch the vellum to the card, making a feature of the stitches. You can machine or hand stitch – although hand stitching is easier if you pierce needle holes before you start sewing.
- Make a vellum wrap. Place a folded piece of vellum around your card, use double-sided tape to attach the vellum down the left-hand edge of the card, near the spine, and wrap a ribbon lengthways to hide the tape.
- Punch matching holes through the top of a vellum shape and your card blank, and tie the vellum shape to the card with ribbon. This works best if the shape is cut from heavy vellum.
- Use silicone glue or dry adhesives such as double-sided tape, rather than PVA; the water content in PVA or tacky glue will wrinkle the vellum.
- It is possible to buy vellum adhesive, although many still show through. Scotch Vellum Tape is one of the most effective.

Parchment

Unless you are purchasing genuine sheep or goat skin parchment (which is very expensive), two different types of paper are generally referred to as parchment in the card making world. One type is a heavier version of vellum, used for Pergamano work (see chapter 6). The other type is an opaque paper with a mottled effect, designed to resemble ancient parchment and often used for printing out certificates.

Mulberry paper

There are many different types of handmade paper, although mulberry paper is the one most commonly used in card making.

About mulberry paper

Mulberry paper is made from the bark of the mulberry tree, and the long fibres give the paper its characteristic feathery texture. When you find mulberry paper in a craft shop or online, it's likely to be a lightweight paper similar to tissue – although mulberry paper is also made in heavier weights. Mulberry tissue paper has a light, delicate texture with a translucent quality. It comes in many different colours, and it's also available with added gold or silver strands, flecks of gold or silver and small motifs such as paper hearts embedded in the paper. You can also buy mulberry paper printed with patterns or motifs.

'Mulberry tissue paper has a light, delicate texture with a translucent quality.'

www.craftcreations.com has an excellent selection of mulberry and other handmade papers, and the photographs on their website are good-quality representations. As well as regular and patterned mulberry, they also have lace paper (a stunning mulberry paper with loose, random holes giving a lacy look), abaca paper (a mulberry paper with extra fibres for added texture) and terrazzo (a mix of mulberry and bamboo, with coloured flecks to give a marbled look).

Tearing mulberry

Mulberry tissue is great for tearing. The fibres give a beautiful, lacy edge that adds visual interest to a card and complements a cut edge. You can tear mulberry paper randomly by carefully pulling the fibres apart. Alternatively, you can create a controlled tear by wetting a thin paintbrush with water and painting wet lines to tear along. The dampened fibres pull apart easily and you can tear out quite complex shapes using this method. Try hearts, flowers, stars and simple teddy bear shapes.

Cutting and sticking mulberry

Because of the rough texture of mulberry and other handmade papers, double-sided tape does not work very well. Regular PVA glue is good for sticking down mulberry tissue – and if you stick white over a coloured card, the colour combines with the white fibres to create a misted effect. If you want to punch mulberry shapes, use mulberry covered card; the paper is too delicate to punch effectively by itself, and may even jam your punch. It's also hard to cut mulberry with a guillotine, craft blade or rotary trimmer. If you want a cut edge, use scissors – although the torn edge looks so effective, you probably won't want to cut mulberry any other way!

Some other handmade papers

Many other substances are used for making handmade paper, including banana, lokta, jute, hemp and recycled paper. Handmade paper comes in a variety of different weights and textures. Some handmade papers have petals, leaves and fibres embedded during the manufacturing process to give a natural, speckled look.

'Scrapbooking paper is a great source of basic patterns such as spots, stripes, ginghams, checks and flourishes.'

Make this

Make a panel-shaped card topper by covering a rectangle of coloured card with white mulberry (make sure that every part of the card is covered with glue or the mulberry will bubble). Fold the mulberry over the edges of the card and stick to the back of the card, to make a neat finish. Place the panel between two paper towels and put under a heavy book to dry flat – checking occasionally to make sure the panel isn't gluing itself to the paper towels. Twist thin white ribbon around the panel and scatter with small white punched daisies. Use a small circle punch to make centres for the daisies, choosing a colour that matches the colour of the card panel.

Patterned paper (scrapbooking paper)

There is a huge range of patterned papers available. Many patterned papers are designed for scrapbooking and come in the square 12" by 12" size (30cm by 30cm). Scrapbooking paper usually has a pattern on both sides so it can be displayed within the plastic pockets of a scrapbooking album. Although not cheap, scrapbooking paper is great for backgrounds, matting and layering and cutting out images for cards – and a little goes a long way unless you are making jumbo cards!

Most scrapbook paper manufacturers are American. Basic Grey, Bo Bunny, DCWV (short for Die Cuts With a View), 7 Gypsies and Authentique are just some of the companies that produce good-quality papers. Scrapbooking paper is a great source of basic patterns such as spots, stripes, ginghams, checks and flourishes.

Many scrapbook papers are themed (holiday, baby girl or boy, Christmas, Halloween, motifs for men, vintage, florals and so on). This makes them a useful source if you want to create a specific card. Scrapbook papers also tend to come in collections, with colours, background patterns, shapes, motifs and themes that work well together. This is very useful if you are not particularly confident about matching colours, patterns and images.

Make this – a card from scrapbook paper

To make a quick and simple card, buy a scrapbooking sheet with a large floral pattern and a matching background sheet. Matt and layer with the background paper and a second paper, such as mulberry tissue in a complementary colour (see chapter 10 for details on matting and layering). Cut out three of the flowers and arrange in a triangle against the background. Finish off with a sentiment and a few accents such as flat backed pearls, ribbon and/or a bow.

Other card and paper finishes

Apart from the categories we have already looked at, there are many more types of card and paper:

- Glossy – Glossy card or paper has a smooth, shiny coloured surface, but it does not reflect in the same way as mirri card.
- Shimmer – As its name suggests, shimmer paper shimmers and changes colour when you move it. The surface of the paper has a grainy texture, which adds to its iridescence.

- Marbled – Marbled paper or card has beautiful, random swirls of colour. Genuine handmade marbled paper is stunning but very expensive. It's not difficult to make your own with special marbling inks – well worth trying if you like the unique effect of marbled paper.
- Foiled – Foiled paper or card has a metallic foiled pattern (usually in gold or silver). The pattern can range from simple dots to elaborate swirls. Some papers have foiled accents that pick out the elements of a printed pattern.
- Metallic crinkle – This is a beautiful and unusual paper. Although quite thick, it is a soft paper that looks as though it has been crumpled up and then smoothed out. The surface has a leathery feel, and it comes in a muted gold and silver. Perfect for Christmas cards!
- Embossed – Embossed means that the card or paper has a slightly raised pattern, and it can include textured paper (such as hammered), the embossed pearlescent card mentioned previously, two-tone paper with a coloured background and gold or silver embossed pattern and paper embossed with an animal skin texture.
- Holographic – Holographic paper or card is patterned with sparkly, rainbow holographic images. It works well for children's and teenagers' cards.

'Browsing through card and paper options and deciding what to buy is one of the joys of card making.'

Enjoy your papers!

Browsing through card and paper options and deciding what to buy is one of the joys of card making. Many card makers joke about having two sets of every paper and card sample – one to craft with, and one to stroke and admire!

Sheet material

Sheet material is anything flat that doesn't fit into the paper or card category:

Acetate

Acetate is a transparent, colourless sheet material that can be used whenever you want to create the effect of glass.

Using acetate

Acetate is an essential ingredient for making shaker cards, and it also looks effective stuck inside an aperture to represent the glass in a frame (see chapter 1 for more on shaker cards and aperture card blanks). Acetate can also be used as a card blank or a card wrap:

- To make a so-called card blank from acetate, simply cut and fold into shape and stick your embellishments on the front of the acetate. Stick a paper shape on the inside to write on.
- To make an acetate card wrap, use the same technique as that for making a vellum wrap – see page 43. If you wish, you can decorate the acetate wrap with subtle patterns, such as stamped shapes.
- An acetate wrap can also be curved across the front of the card to create a beautiful and unusual effect for a special card. For a demonstration, go to the video tutorials section of www.card making-magic.com and click on Acetate front card tutorial.

Decorating acetate

Acetate can be decorated in a number of ways, including stamping, stencilling and glittering. It also makes a beautiful background for an outline sticker, particularly if you colour in the sections to create a stained glass window effect. For specific instructions on how to stamp, stencil, glitter and apply colour to acetate, see the following chapters.

Printing on acetate

You can print onto acetate, as long as you use acetate that is suitable for an inkjet printer. Printable acetate has a rough side and a smooth side. Make sure you print onto the rough side and use a normal printer setting.

Sticking acetate

PVA glues don't work very well on acetate as it is non-porous and smooth. Like vellum, acetate can be challenging to stick because any adhesive will show through. Double-sided tape or sticky dots work well as an adhesive, and you can cover the glue patch with an embellishment. For example, if you stick a heart-shaped embellishment on the front of an acetate card blank, stick an identical shape directly behind it (on the left hand inside of the card when opened).

You can also use brads (see chapter 7) to attach acetate to your card, and artistically placed staples are becoming more and more popular as a means of fixing sheet materials.

Angel Hair

Angel Hair looks like flat candy floss. It comes in a range of colours, and some Angel Hair has added gold and silver strands or glitter. Angel Hair makes a beautiful and unusual texture for matting and layering, backgrounds and sticking behind apertures.

Foam sheets

'Foam sheets make fun and colourful embellishment for children's cards.'

Foam sheets are thin sheets of spongy, coloured foam. They are easy to cut and also work well with most paper punches. Foam sheets make fun and colourful embellishment for children's cards. You can buy self-adhesive foam, but it sticks so well with tacky PVA that it doesn't seem worth the extra expense. Save scraps and offcuts of foam to make your own foam pads for decoupage (see chapter 7). Simply cut the foam into small shapes and use tacky PVA to glue them between your decoupage layers.

Flock and Vivelle sheets

Flock sheets have a velvety texture. They are self-adhesive and can be cut with scissors or die cutting machines. Vivelle sheets are similar to flock, but they have a felt rather than a velvet texture. Dark green Vivelle makes a good baize surface for a snooker-themed man's card (see also flock powder in chapter 8).

Craft CDs

There is a huge selection of craft CDs available. Each CD contains a range of patterned papers, images, sentiments and, in some cases, card shapes and digi-stamps. Crafting CDs allow you to manipulate colours, patterns, images and sizes on the screen, before printing them out. This gives you a massive number of choices, with many CDs offering a thousand or more possibilities. The downside is the cost of printing. To get a pleasing result, you need to have a reliable printer, a steady supply of inks and good-quality printing or photo paper.

Craft designer Joanna Sheen sells a wide range of CDs – including her *House Mouse* collection, which is charming and witty without being twee. Her website includes tips on printing from CDs, lots of card-making ideas and designs, and a forum where you can ask for advice from the many experienced members (including Joanna herself if she happens to be online!) Her website address is www.joannasheen.co.uk.

'Crafting CDs allow you to manipulate colours, patterns, images and sizes on the screen, before printing them out.'

Summing Up

- The thickness of paper or card is measured in grams per square metre (gsm). The higher the number, the heavier the paper.
- There is a huge variety of different patterns, colours, textures and types of paper and card to choose from.
- Some papers and cards work better with dry adhesive, and some can be used with any type of adhesive.
- Handmade paper such as mulberry tissue is great for tearing. If you want to cut mulberry tissue, use scissors rather than a paper trimmer, guillotine or craft knife.
- Sheet material such as acetate, Angel Hair and Vivelle can be used to create interesting effects on your cards.
- Crafting CDs offer a massive choice of background papers and images – although you do need good-quality paper, plenty of ink and a reliable printer.

Chapter Four

Stamping With Ink

Stamping images with a stamp and ink pad is a popular and versatile card-making technique. Over the last few years, the choice of stamps and ink pads has exploded into a dizzying number of different possibilities. In this chapter we explore what is available and look at which types of stamp, ink pad and cardstock are needed to create different effects.

Stamping basics - stamps

Stamping involves pressing a stamp with a raised or etched pattern onto an ink pad, and holding it down on card or paper to leave an inked impression. There are many different types of stamp you can use in card making:

Wood mounted rubber stamps

These are the traditional crafting stamps. The stamping surface is made of red or grey rubber and mounted onto a wooden block. The wooden block has a picture of the stamped image so you can see what you are buying.

Wood mounted rubber stamps are tough and long lasting. They will even withstand heat if you want to create impressions by pressing them into molten ultra-thick embossing powder (see chapter 6). They are quite expensive, but they can be used again and again – as long as they are well looked after.

Unmounted rubber stamps

Rubber stamps are increasingly sold unmounted, without the wooden block. This makes them cheaper and easier to store, as they take up less room. Unmounted rubber stamps are often supplied in sheets. Use good-quality, sharp scissors to cut out each stamp – and aim to cut as close to the edge of the stamp as possible, without cutting into the image itself.

Unmounted rubber stamps need to be put on a mount before you can use them. The easiest way to do this is with a clear acrylic mounting block and a substance called EZ Mount. EZ Mount is a foam sheet that is sticky on one side and clingy on the other. To use, you simply stick the rubber stamp to the sticky side, cut round it and attach the clingy side to the acrylic block. When you have finished stamping, unpeel the stamp from the block and store until you next need it. If the clingy side of the EZ Mount stops sticking to the acrylic block, wash it in warm soapy water to get rid of dust and any other residue.

'Photopolymer stamps are the most reliable, giving a consistently crisp image. Acrylic stamps can be a little more variable in quality and silicone stamps tend to be poor quality.'

Apart from providing a quick and easy way of sticking rubber stamps to a block, the foam layer in EZ Mount improves the quality of the stamped image. Joanna Sheen sells both EZ Mount and a wide range of clear acrylic blocks in different sizes (www.joannasheen.co.uk). She also has a useful YouTube tutorial on how to use EZ Mount, entitled 'Joanna Sheen – Unmounted Rubber Stamps and EZ Mount Foam'. For more about acrylic mounting blocks, see the next page.

Clear stamps

As their name suggests, clear stamps are colourless and transparent. They are made of photopolymer, acrylic or silicone. Photopolymer stamps are the most reliable, giving a consistently crisp image. Acrylic stamps can be a little more variable in quality and silicone stamps tend to be poor quality. Designer Barbara Gray of Claritystamp (www.claritystamp.co.uk) is the originator of clear stamps, and she produces excellent quality polymer stamps, as do Woodware (www.woodware.co.uk).

Clear stamps are sold unmounted, sometimes as individual stamps, but more often in a sheet. As with the unmounted rubber stamp, the clear stamp has to be mounted on an acrylic block. The back of the clear stamp is static and will cling to the acrylic block without the need for an adhesive. If the stamp starts to lose its clinginess, wash it in warm soapy water.

Once the stamp is finished with and cleaned, it can be replaced on the backing sheet supplied with the sheet of stamps.

Acrylic blocks

An acrylic block is a clear, flattish cuboid that comes in various sizes. As already mentioned, Joanna Sheen sells a good selection on her crafting website. If you find the cuboid shape hard to hold, Claritystamp do an acrylic block mount with a specially designed, award-winning handle. Another popular variation on the acrylic block is the Crafter's Companion Rock-A-Block. The Rock-A-Block is bevelled so that you can gently roll the stamp forwards. This action prevents smudging and helps to ensure that the whole image is printed. It's also easier for crafters with dexterity problems to 'rock' rather than press down.

'With clear stamps on an acrylic block, you can see exactly where you are placing your stamp.'

Rubber and clear stamps – the pros and cons

- Clear stamps are usually a bit cheaper than unmounted rubber stamps – and a lot cheaper than rubber stamps with a wooden handle.
- With clear stamps on an acrylic block, you can see exactly where you are placing your stamp. This is a little harder with a rubber stamp on an acrylic block and much harder with a rubber stamp on a wooden block.
- If you have a large acrylic block, you can place several separate clear stamps on the surface to make a pattern.
- Solvent-based inks such as StazOn are too harsh for clear stamps, but are fine for rubber stamps.
- Rubber stamps tend to give a crisper, clearer image than clear stamps – although the quality of clear stamps has improved over the last few years. As with most crafting materials, you get what you pay for.

- Rubber stamps are more durable than clear stamps. They can withstand being used in molten embossing powder and tend to last longer than clear stamps.
- Wooden mounted rubber stamps, although expensive, are beautiful objects in their own right.

Stamping basics – ink pads

Apart from your collection of stamps, you will need an ink pad – or better still, several ink pads! Different types of inks have different purposes, so you need to make sure you've got the right ink pad for the job in hand.

The following is a general survey of what is available:

Dye-based ink pads

Dye-based inks are good for general stamping and also suitable for children to use. The ink pad itself is made from firm felt rather than squishy sponge – which means that you are less likely to swamp your stamp with ink, or get ink on the edge of your stamp block.

Dye-based ink dries quickly, and it gives a clear, crisp, detailed image. Some dye-based inks are waterproof once they are dry, and some are not. If you want to use a water-based colouring medium on your stamped images, choose a waterproof ink such as Ranger Archival.

Because dye-based ink soaks into the surface of the paper or card, it can seem to disappear if you use it on dark paper. You will get the clearest and brightest result if you use it on white or pale coloured card. Most dye-based inks also fade over time, and because they are quite a thin ink, they tend to look brighter on the pad than on the stamped image. Good-quality ink pad manufacturers usually sell re-inkers.

Some good-quality dye-based ink pads include Adirondack, Memento, Ranger Archival, Ranger Big and Juicy and Tim Holtz Distress inks.

Pigment-based ink pads

Pigment inks are thicker in consistency than dye inks – which makes them slow-drying. Unlike dye-based inks, pigment inks do not soak into the surface of the card. This makes the pigment ink your best choice if you want to produce a crisp image on an absorbent paper.

Pigment inks tend to produce a more vibrant print than dye inks. However, some of them are unsuitable for stamping on glossy or coated paper surfaces, as the ink simply won't dry (one exception to this is the Brilliance ink pad, which will dry on glossy surfaces given time). Because they dry slowly, pigment inks are suitable for heat embossing – and you can use them on a glossy or coated surface in this instance, as the heat embossing process fixes the ink onto the surface.

Pigment inks have a sponge pad, rather than a felt pad. For this reason, you need to ink your stamp with care as it's easy for the stamp to sink into the sponge and become saturated. Because of their thicker consistency, the colour of the ink on the pad is fairly similar to the colour you will get on your stamped image.

Some good-quality pigment ink pads include Brilliance, Versacolor, Adirondack Pigment Inks and Encore. The Brilliance range includes pearlescent colours and all the Encore colours have a metallic shimmer.

'Solvent-based ink pads can be used on any surface – which makes them a reliable choice if you want to stamp on acetate, glass or metal.'

Solvent-based ink pads

Solvent-based ink pads can be used on any surface – which makes them a reliable choice if you want to stamp on acetate, glass or metal, as well as all types of paper and card. Solvent inks are opaque and tend to have a chemically smell. They are not suitable for children to use.

Solvent inks are best avoided with clear stamps. It's hard to clean off the ink with anything other than a specialist solvent ink remover, which damages the polymer. The cleaner is fine for rubber stamps.

The most common and popular solvent ink pad is StazOn. It's suitable for porous and semi-porous surfaces, including plastic, metal, glass, acrylic, cellophane, ceramic, leather and coated paper or card. It comes in a good range of colours and has a milder smell than the average solvent-based ink.

Embossing ink pads

Any slow-drying ink pads, such as the pigment inks, can be used for heat embossing – but an embossing ink pad is specially designed for this particular technique (see chapter 6 for everything you need to know about heat embossing). Embossing ink pads are extra sticky and either clear or lightly tinted – which means you end up with the pure colour of the embossing powder on your image. If you want to see where you have stamped, go for a tinted pad.

Clear ink pads can also be used for stamping a water mark on dark paper, or brushing over with chalk (page 63) or mica powder (page 64).

Some popular embossing ink pads include Versamark, Tim Holtz Distress Clear Embossing Ink Pad and Tsukineko's Emboss. Versamark comes in both large and small sizes, and Emboss is available in tinted as well as clear.

Chalk ink pads

Chalk ink is an opaque pigment ink that dries to a chalky, matte finish. Even though they are pigment-based, chalk inks will dry on a glossy surface – and they also blend well. Chalk ink pads often come in small sizes. Two of the most popular types are Versamagic Chalk Inks and ColorBox Fluid Chalk. The Versamagic chalk ink is available in a dewdrop shape and the ColorBox Fluid Chalk comes in the shape of a cat's eye. Both these shapes are surprisingly useful for getting into corners and inking up just one section of a stamp.

Try this – chalk resist images

Stamp an image with Versamark clear embossing ink and when dry, dab over with two or three chalk inks. The clear Versamark image will resist the chalk ink and show through the coloured background.

Stamping basics – card, paper and other surfaces

Paper, card and other sheet materials have a major effect on the end result of your stamping. Not only do you need a surface that will work with your overall card design, you also have to work out which inkpad and colouring technique is best for your chosen card or paper.

Stamping on plain card and paper

You can stamp on any kind of paper or card, but for basic stamping it's advisable to work on cardstock rather than paper. Paper warps and wrinkles more easily, particularly if you plan to decorate your stamped images with water-based colour.

With card, as with most crafting supplies, the general rule is – you get what you pay for. Buying specialist stamping cardstock from reputable stamping companies is the safest bet when you are starting out. Alternatively, try the brand recommended by an online or high street craft store. For example, The Craft Barn (www.thecraftbarn.co.uk) sells a brilliant white, super smooth cardstock that has good reviews from its customers.

You can stamp on any colour of cardstock, and this can be particularly effective if you are not planning to colour in your stamped image. However, if you want to use coloured pens, chalks, water colour pencils or paints, they generally stand out better on white or ivory card.

Trying cheaper cardstock

Once you are experienced with stamping, try exploring different brands of card. Some experienced stampers manage to find a cheap cardstock that gives them good results.

Stamping on hammer card

Smooth cardstock will give you the crispest stamped image, but it's worth experimenting with hammer card if you like the texture. Because of the bumps and valleys, it's challenging to get a complete print – but at least some of your attempts should be usable. Hammer card also works well for creating random stamped backgrounds.

Stamping on glossy and pearlescent card

Stamping on card with a glossy or pearlescent surface looks good, as long as you use the right ink. The challenge with stamping onto glossy surfaces is getting the ink to dry – which means that most pigment inks are best avoided. Try the dye-based ink Memento. The solvent-based StazOn also works well, although you can't colour in with alcohol based pens if you use StazOn.

'Stamping on card with a glossy or pearlescent surface looks good, as long as you use the right ink.'

Stamping on vellum

Stamping on vellum creates a lovely effect, but you need to press down with care as the smooth surface of the vellum makes it slippery. Vellum also tends to stick to the ink pad; hold the vellum down as you lift off the ink pad to avoid smudging the image. As the surface of vellum is non-absorbent, the ink will take some time to dry. Brilliance or Ranger Archival ink pads both work well on vellum.

Stamping on handmade papers

Stamping on handmade paper is similar to stamping on hammer card, as the surface tends to be uneven. Some handmade papers are also very absorbent, resulting in a stamped image that bleeds as the ink soaks into the fibres of the paper. Ink with a wetter consistency tends to work better than a quick-drying ink as it gives a stronger image

With so many different types of handmade paper available, the best approach is to experiment with your ink pads. As a general rule, a block-style stamp gives better results than one with lots of fine detail. The rough surface of the paper also works well with natural images such as flowers, leaves and shells, or simple, bold designs with an ethnic feel.

Stamping on patterned papers

Some great effects can be achieved by stamping on patterned paper. Go for paper with a subtle pattern so that the stamped images show up – although, as always, there are no rules and you may find that a bold stamp with dark ink looks effective on a strongly patterned paper.

Choose an ink pad colour that complements the colour of the paper. The ink doesn't have to be black – although it's a good idea to have a try out, to make sure that the colour and intensity of the ink work on the paper. You also need to choose the right type of ink for the paper surface, particularly if you are using a patterned scrapbook paper with a semi-gloss surface.

Try this – three colour stamping

Choose a subtly patterned paper in three different but complementary colours. Stamp an identical image on each colour, cut out and use the three images as the focal point for your card design. A simple technique, but surprisingly effective!

How to stamp

Successful stamping is dependent on the following:

- Good-quality stamps and ink pad
- The right type of cardstock or paper to achieve the effect you are after
- The right type of ink for the stamping surface
- Applying the ink to the stamp in an even layer
- Keeping the stamp still on the paper

- Lifting off the stamp without smudging the image

Follow these steps:

1. Choose the right work surface for you. Some card makers like to do their stamping on a hard table surface – whereas others prefer a softer surface, such as a specially designed stamping mat.
2. Ink your stamp. Keep the stamp on the table and take the ink pad to the stamp, tapping gently all over the surface to apply the ink. If your ink pad is made of sponge, be careful the stamp doesn't become engulfed. Make sure you haven't inadvertently got ink on the edges of the block, or your stamped image will have a ghostly frame.
3. Put the lid back on your ink pad – and get into the habit of doing this straight away so the ink doesn't dry up.
4. Press the stamp down on the paper with a firm, even pressure. If the stamp is large, you need to apply pressure to all the parts with your fingertips. Some crafters find it easier to stand up when they work with large stamps.
5. Take care not to wobble or move the stamp while pressing down as this will blur the image. Be particularly careful if you are stamping on a glossy, slippery surface.
6. Lift the stamp off the paper in one smooth movement – and leave the image to dry before colouring or cutting out.

'Practice makes perfect, and the more stamping you do, the better your results will be.'

Play with a new stamp to get a feel for it. Practice makes perfect, and the more stamping you do, the better your results will be.

Conditioning new stamps

Some new stamps still have manufacturing residue on their surface. If you find that your new stamp is not giving a very clear impression, you may need to condition the stamp by removing this residue. Try washing with soapy water, rubbing over the stamp with a white pencil eraser or using a stamp cleaner (see page 68 for more on cleaning stamps).

Colouring your stamped images

Once you have stamped your image and left it to dry, you can either leave it as it is, or you can colour it in. There are various ways of colouring a stamped image – and you also need to go for colouring techniques that work with both the paper surface and the type of ink you have chosen.

Pens

Pens are the easiest way of applying colour to the different sections of your stamped images. Alcohol pens such as ProMarkers result in a smooth, transparent finish that looks very professional. For metallic, sparkly, fluorescent, pearlescent or glazed effects, try the Sakura Gelly Roll range of gel pens.

Because the ink in ProMarkers is alcohol-based, they tend to smudge when used with other solvent-based inks (such as StazOn). If you plan to colour in your stamped images with alcohol ink pens, make sure you choose a water-based ink pad. Letraset, who make ProMarkers, recommend the Tsukineko Memento ink pad.

For more about different types of pens and how to use them, see chapter 8.

'Alcohol pens such as ProMarkers result in a smooth, transparent finish that looks very professional.'

Chalks

Chalks are a little harder to control than pens, and you get a soft smudgy look rather than a sharp, crisp finish. There are no rules as to when you should use chalk or pens to colour in stamps – but chalks work particularly well for simple, organic images such as flowers, butterflies or a loosely detailed pattern.

To colour in a stamped image with chalk, gently rub the chalk over different parts of the stamp. Don't worry about the colour overlapping the edges of your image – that's all part of the effect. Remember that you may need to spray fixative over a chalked stamped image, to stop the colours from smudging. For more on chalks and how to use them, see chapter 8.

Try this – chalking a stamped image

Use a Versamark ink pad to stamp an image. While the ink is still wet, gently dab chalk over the stamped image to create soft, misty lines. The chalk will not need fixing, as the ink glues it to the paper.

Water colour pencils

Water colour pencils can be used in the same way as ordinary coloured pencils – but once you have lightly coloured in your stamped image, you can brush over the colour with a wet paint brush to create the effect of water colour paint.

Water colour pencils can only be used to colour images stamped with waterproof inks, such as StazOn or Ranger Archival.

Water brushes

If you plan to use water brushing regularly in your crafting, it's well worth investing in a water brush. This is a hollow plastic tube with a brush at one end. The tube is filled with water and gently squeezed to send a steady flow of water into the brush.

Mica powders and paints

Mica powders can be mixed with water and applied to your stamped images with a fine paint brush (see chapter 8 for everything you need to know about mica powders). The sparkly sheen of mica paints adds a special touch to stamping projects. You can also use mica powder in a similar way to glitter. Stamp an image using a Versamark ink pad or Ranger Perfect Medium, and use a soft, dry brush to apply dry mica powder across the stamped image. The powder sticks to the ink, creating a beautiful shimmery image. It's a good idea to finish off with a fixative, to make sure the powder doesn't smudge. Black or dark coloured card brings out the colours of mica powders, making them glow.

Glitter and glitter glue

Sparkly glitter or glitter glue looks pretty on a stamped image. For details on how to colour in your stamped images with glitter, see chapter 8.

Water colour paints

Applied with a fine brush, water colour paints make yet another option for colouring your stamped images. If you are new to art and craft, it's probably best not to start off with water colours. Stick to easier methods such as alcohol pens, gel pens or watercolour pencils.

Some more stamping techniques

Once you have mastered stamping as a basic technique, there are lots of exciting things you can do with your new found skills:

'Sparkly glitter or glitter glue looks pretty on a stamped image.'

Stamping on acetate

Stamping and colouring images on clear acetate can create some fabulous stained glass effects. There is, however, a conundrum when it comes to working on acetate:

- A solvent-based ink pad, such as StazOn, is the best choice for stamping on acetate.
- Alcohol pens, such as ProMarkers, produce beautiful jewel-like colours on acetate.
- You can't use solvent-based inks and alcohol pens together!

The way round this problem is to stamp on the acetate with StazOn, and then colour in the sections of the stamped image on the *back* of the acetate. This means that the alcohol ink doesn't ever come into contact with the solvent-based ink.

You may find that stronger, brighter coloured pens show up better on acetate than softer, pastel shades. Experiment to see which colours work best with your particular set of pens, before going ahead with your card design.

As an alternative colour medium, the Sakura Glaze pens can also be used on acetate – and they create a raised translucent effect once dry. If you like creating coloured stamped images on acetate, it's well worth investing in a set of these beautiful pens.

Stamping different intensities

The more you stamp, the more faded the image becomes as the ink gets used up. If you are stamping an image as the central embellishment for your card design, you will want to use a freshly inked stamp. You can, however, make good use of different colour intensities to create quick and easy backgrounds.

Choose a stamp with a simple outline and an inkpad with a light tone, and stamp randomly – only re-inking when the image disappears altogether. This will give you a 3D effect, with stronger images appearing to pop out of the paper and shadowy images appearing to recede. Try stamping some images off the edge of the paper to create a more natural look.

Repeat stamping

Use a stamped image repeatedly to create a line or pattern of identical images. This is a useful technique for making a border. A clear stamp on an acrylic block enables you to see where you are placing each image – although you may need to measure and make pencil markings to create even spaces between the images.

Try this – stamped border strips

Stamp a row of small, simple images on card. Colour the images or leave them plain, depending on the effect you want to create. Using a paper trimmer or craft knife, cut the images into strips and stick them along the top and/or bottom of a card, or down the sides. Have a session of creating stamped border strips to save for future cards.

Making a patchwork stamped image

This technique involves making up a stamped image from different papers. Choose your stamp, for example, a cute cartoon girl. Choose the papers you want to work with and stamp the image of the girl onto each paper. Cut out her skirt from one paper, her top from another and so on. For a natural look, stamp one image on white card and colour in the face, hands and legs using skin tone alcohol ink pens. Stick all the cut-out pieces together to create a complete patchwork image of the girl. As you become more adept, experiment with different thicknesses of paper or card to create a 3D effect. For example, sturdy handmade paper can be used to add bulk to the clothes.

This technique also works well with flower stamps. For example, choose pink pearlescent paper for the petals, cream hammer paper for the stamens and a Bazzill Basics green textured paper for the leaves.

3D stamped images

Stamp your image on card and colour it in. Cut round the outer edge of the stamped outline and use foam pads to attach it to your card blank. This will give the image a raised, three-dimensional look.

Masking

Masking is a simple but ingenious technique that enables you to overlap your stamped images and make them look more natural:

1. Stamp your image onto card.
2. Re-ink your stamp and stamp onto a post-it note, making sure that some of the sticky edge is included in the stamp.
3. Cut out the stamped image from the post-it note and stick it exactly over the stamped image on the card.
4. Re-ink your stamp (or ink up a new stamp) and stamp the image so that it partly overlaps the mask.

5. Remove the mask to reveal how the first stamped image appears to be positioned in front of the second.

Caring for your stamps

Rubber stamps will last a lifetime if they are cared for. Clear stamps tend to be less robust, but a good-quality clear stamp can still be used over and over again – as long as you look after it.

Cleaning stamps

Make sure you clean your stamps after every use. Apart from not wanting old ink to contaminate your images, dried ink will also clog up the stamp and give a smudged, blurry result.

'Rubber stamps will last a lifetime if they are cared for.'

Rubber stamps

If your rubber stamp is wood mounted, avoid soaking it as this will damage the wood. To remove ink from the rubber surface, try the following:

- Stamp cleaner – Specialist rubber stamp cleaners can be purchased from craft stores, or online.
- Baby wipes – These are useful for cleaning stamps, but make sure they don't contain lanolin or alcohol, as both these substances will attack the rubber.
- Soapy water – Washing-up liquid in warm water and a soft toothbrush will remove most inks.
- StazOn All Purpose Cleaner – This is necessary for cleaning solvent inks such as StazOn from your rubber stamps.

Clear stamps

Clear stamps need gentler treatment than rubber stamps. Stick to water, a little mild washing-up liquid and a soft toothbrush. If you want to use a stamp cleaner, go for one designed especially for clear stamps, such as Inkssentials Clear Stamp Cleaner.

Stained or dirty?

Bear in mind that stained is different from dirty. A stained stamp may not look so pretty but it won't affect your stamping – as long as there is no actual ink residue on the surface of the stamp.

Storing stamps

Storing your stamps correctly will also help them to last:

Rubber stamps

Make sure your stamps are completely dry before putting them away, and store them out of sunlight. Avoid stacking rubber stamps as this might damage the surface of the rubber. Make sure unmounted rubber stamps are stored flat, to prevent them from buckling.

Many crafters store stamps backed with EZ Mount in empty CD cases – first removing the plastic CD holder. It's worth being organised and labelling each CD case with a code. Make a stamped image for each stamp, note which CD case it is in and store the coded images in a folder. As your collection builds, this system will make it much easier to find what you are looking for.

Clear stamps

Clear stamps can be stored on their original backing sheet, and placed in a folder with clear plastic pockets. They can also be stored in empty CD cases, and some are sold with their own CD-style cases. As with unmounted rubber stamps, code your storage system so you don't lose track of what you have.

You can also buy special unmounted stamp storage systems. Claritystamp sell their own Clarity Binder for storing stamps and Joanna Sheen sells an EZ Mount Binder for stamps backed with EZ Mount.

Summing Up

- The basic materials you need for stamping are a rubber or clear stamp, an ink pad and paper or card to stamp on to.
- Some rubber stamps are mounted on wood, but an unmounted stamp needs to be mounted on an acrylic block. Clear stamps cling to the block, but rubber stamps need to be adhered with a substance such as EZ Mount.
- There are different types of ink pad, including dye-based, pigment-based and solvent-based ink. You need to choose the right type of ink for your stamping surface.
- You can stamp onto lots of different surfaces. Good-quality, smooth white card will give you the best result, but you can also stamp onto coated papers, vellum and acetate – as long as you use the right kind of ink.
- There are many different techniques for colouring in your stamped images, including alcohol pens, chalks, glitter, mica powders, water colour pencils and water colour paints.
- Once you have mastered the basics of stamping, you can use your new skill in lots of creative ways. Masking, repeat stamping, making backgrounds and patchwork stamping are just some of the possibilities.

Chapter Five

Peel-Offs and Paper Punches

It's surprising how many effects you can create with a peel-off sticker and a paper punch. No card maker should be without these two fabulous techniques – and in this chapter, we look at what is available and how they can be used.

'"Peel-off" is the term most commonly used in the card making world for a sticker.'

Different types of peel-offs and stickers

'Peel-off' is the term most commonly used in the card-making world for a sticker. Peel-offs usually come on a coated sheet, enabling you to take off what you want to use and save the rest for later. There are many different types of peel-off and sticker:

Outline stickers

Outline stickers consist of just an outline, as if the motif has been drawn with a pen. If you think of the leading in a stained glass window, this gives you a rough idea of how an outline sticker is structured. Once the outline sticker has been placed on card or paper, it looks as though it has been embossed onto the surface of the card. If the shapes within the peel-off are decorated with care, it takes a crafter to tell that a particular effect has been created with a sticker.

Outline stickers come in a huge range of motifs and patterns, including flowers, stars, candles, cupcakes, butterflies, dragonflies, dresses, shoes, gifts, Celtic designs, art deco designs, medallions and themes such as football, wedding and religious. Anita's Outline Stickers are a good brand to look out for. They are excellent quality and they offer a great variety to choose from. You will also find a huge selection of peel-offs at www.craftcreations.com.

Outline peel-offs usually come in metallic gold or silver, although you can also get them in white, black and other colours. Smaller peel-offs are easy to manage, but larger ones need a bit of care. Use a sharp pokey tool (see chapter 2) or the tip of a craft knife to lift the peel-off from the backing paper. Because it is only an outline, the shape can stretch and distort as you lift it off. Give it a few moments in mid-air to 'relax' back into shape, before carefully laying it down on the paper or card background. If you rest the sticker gently on the paper, you can lift it up and reposition it as necessary – although you can only do this a couple of times before it loses its 'stick'. When you are sure you have it in the right place, press it down with the fingertips.

Picture stickers

'Picture stickers are great for children's card making.'

Picture stickers are, as their name suggests, coloured pictures with a sticky backing. Picture stickers often feature popular characters, such as the cute Forever Friends bears, and they make an easy-to-use embellishment for a card. You can either put your design efforts into creating an interesting background for the sticker, or keep things simple if you want to make a card in a hurry. Picture stickers are also great for children's card making.

If you want to sell your cards, check that there isn't a copyright issue for picture stickers. See chapter 10 for more on copyright.

Borders, frames and corners

Border, frame and corner peel-offs are very useful to keep in your crafting box:

- Border peel-offs come as thin strips of gold or silver, or fancy designs such as chains, Greek key, zigzags, interlinked hearts, stitching or wavy lines. You will need pencil markings to make sure you get your border peel-off straight. For example, if you want a border strip a centimetre in from the edge of your card, use a ruler to measure and mark the top and bottom points. Lift the border from the backing sheet with a pokey tool, place it so that it joins the two marks on your card and trim the overlapping ends. It's a good idea to put a tiny dot of tacky PVA glue under each end of the border, to make sure it doesn't peel away from the card.

- Frame peel-offs are mostly based on square, rectangular, circular or oval, shapes, and they come in straight, wavy and ornate lines. They make a quick, simple and effective way of helping an embellishment to stand out.
- Corner peel-offs are right-angled so that they fit into the corners of the card front. You can get them in a range of different styles and designs, both simple and ornate. Borders and corners often come in matching sets, and you can also buy sheets of peel-offs with both borders and corners.

Words, letters and numbers

From sentiments such as 'Happy Birthday', to single letters and numbers, there is a huge range of words, colours and fonts to choose from. The Anita's peel-off brand has some attractive single letter peel-offs and also a wide range of sentiments. If you want small, plain letters in upper and lower case for building your own words, try www.craftcreations.com and their Gold Label brand of peel-offs.

For more on using peel-offs to create words and sentiments, see chapter 9.

Embroidery peel-offs

Embroidery peel-offs are a testament to the ingenuity of craft manufacturers, and their never-ending ability to introduce new variations on a familiar theme! The embroidery peel-off is an outline sticker mounted on a transparent background, with lines of dots that you can embroider.

Give these a try if you like needlework, as you can achieve some beautiful results. Place the peel-off on paper or thin card. Use a pokey tool or large darning needle to pierce holes in the card and embroider the peel-off using embroidery silks or metallic thread.

Double-sided peel-offs

These peel-offs are transparent and sticky on both sides. To use, position the sticker on your background card and then cover with glitter or metal flakes (see pages 78).

Clear, dome and pebble stickers

Dome stickers are made from a clear, flexible epoxy resin. As the name suggests, they have a domed shape which magnifies whatever is underneath. You can either buy picture stickers covered with a dome, or clear domes that you can stick onto a background of your choice. Dome stickers are sometimes called pebble or bubble stickers. Plain round stickers are particularly useful. Stick them over a circle punched from patterned paper to create a cabochon look.

'Peel-offs are much more than just a sticker that you position on the front of your card.'

Using peel-offs

Peel-offs are much more than just a sticker that you position on the front of your card (although this is always an option if you want something quick and simple). The following section looks at the many different effects you can create with a peel-off. The techniques in this section are all based on outline stickers, as this is the most versatile type of peel-off.

Using outline peel-offs with backing paper

This is one of the simplest techniques for using outline peel-offs. Simply place the outline on coloured or patterned paper or card, and cut round the outer edge of the peel-off. You can either stick the shape straight onto your card blank, or use foam pads to create a 3D effect.

Experiment with using different types of paper and card to back your outline peel-offs. Try white or coloured vellum, mirri card, shimmer paper, handmade paper, glitter card and paper with a subtle pattern. Peel-offs attached to glitter card or handmade paper may need a few dots of tacky glue for extra 'stick'.

If you want to use more than one coloured or patterned paper within your outline sticker, there are two techniques to try:

- Cut out small pieces of different coloured paper to back each section of the outline, and trim around the outer edge of the peel-off to create a neat shape. The lines of the peel-off should hide where the different papers join.
- To create a two-tone effect, stick your outline peel-off onto lightweight backing card and cut it out. Using a craft-knife and working on a cutting mat, cut away the backing card from sections of the peel-off – making sure that you cut inside the lines. Stick the peel-off onto a sheet of card in a contrasting colour so that it shows through the cut-out sections.

Although the results look great, these techniques can be quite fiddly – particularly for designs with small, intricate sections. As an easier and equally effective alternative, you may prefer to use colouring techniques.

Using outline peel-offs with pens

Place an outline sticker on a white background and colour in the sections with pens. To create different effects, try using Sakura gel pens such as Stardust, Moonlight or Metallic. Working on white card will usually give you the brightest results – but this does not mean that you shouldn't experiment with different coloured backgrounds. Once you have completed your colouring in, cut around the outer edge of the outline sticker.

> You can also use chalks, mica powders, loose glitter and glitter glue to colour in your outline stickers. For more on these colouring techniques, see chapter 8

Colouring the peel-off itself

The peel-off itself can also be coloured with ProMarkers or special peel-off marker pens (silver peel-offs work the best).The easiest technique is to colour across the lines of the peel-off while it is still on its backing sheet. Stick to a single colour, or experiment with a range of colours to create a rainbow effect.

Using the inset shapes

As mentioned above, once you have used an outline sticker, you will be left with the inset shapes from the centre of the sections. These too have a number of uses:

Using inset shapes for motifs

The inset shapes from outline stickers can be used to create different images or motifs. Shapes such as circles and ovals can be used to make centres for punched flowers, eyes for animals or spotty borders. Teardrop shapes make good leaves or flower petals – particularly if they are coloured with alcohol pens. Get into the habit of noticing the shapes you are left with, and thinking about how you could use them.

Transferring inset shapes

Once you have used an outline sticker, the entire set of leftover inset shapes can be transferred to card, to create a negative of the outline. This is easy to do if you have an outline sticker transfer sheet. To use the transfer sheet, follow these steps:

- Cut the transfer sheet to size.
- Lay the transfer sheet across the inset shapes on the peel-off backing sheet.
- The inset shapes will stick to the transfer sheet. When you lift off the transfer sheet, the inset shapes will come with it.
- Lay the transfer sheet on your card and burnish over it with a spoon handle. This will transfer the shapes from the transfer sheet to the card.
- Peel the transfer sheet off the card, leaving behind the inset shapes to create a perfect negative of the outline sticker.

You can use Scotch Magic Tape instead of a transfer sheet, although you will need more than one strip if the motif is wider than the tape. If you want to see a visual demonstration of this technique, search for 'Using Dazzles Innies Shapes with Transfer Sheet' on YouTube.

Making a two-tone image

Make a two-tone image with two identical outline stickers in different colours, for example, gold and silver. Follow these steps:

- Lay the gold outline from the gold sticker sheet on your background card.
- Using a pokey tool, pick up one of the silver inset shapes from the silver sheet.
- Place the silver shape inside the corresponding section of the gold outline sticker.
- One by one, transfer each silver inset shape and place them inside the sections on the gold outline sticker.

If you are using a flower sticker, this will give you petals with a gold outline and a silver inset. This technique can look very striking using black and white stickers on a single colour background – such as red or silver.

Use the same technique as above, but colour in the inset shapes with peel-off pens. This will create a multicoloured design when you transfer them to the outline sticker.

'Outline peel-offs look great on clear acetate.'

Using peel-offs on acetate

Outline peel-offs look great on clear acetate. The different sections can be coloured in on the back of the acetate, using alcohol pens such as ProMarkers or Copics (see chapter 8). When you have finished colouring, hold the acetate to the light to make sure you haven't missed a bit. If you use a black outline sticker, the finished result will look like a stained glass window.

Try this – 3D acetate butterfly

Put a butterfly outline sticker on acetate and colour in the sections with alcohol pens. Cut out the butterfly, fold its wings upwards and stick it onto your card with a foam pad to create a 3D effect.

Using peel-offs with vellum

Peel-offs work well with vellum as you can colour in the sections with Sakura gel pens for a pretty effect. You can also turn the vellum over and emboss the back of the peel-off sections with an embossing tool. This creates an effective raised and slightly puffy look. For more on embossing vellum, see chapter 6.

Using peel-offs with gilding flakes

Gilding flakes are small, papery thin flakes of metal in a variety of different metallic colours. You need a black peel-off for this technique as gold and silver outline stickers won't show up against the metallic flakes:

1. Cut out a square or rectangle from a double-sided adhesive sheet.
2. Peel off the protective paper from one side of the square and stick the sheet onto card.
3. Peel off the other sheet of protective paper and stick the black outline sticker carefully in the centre of the adhesive sheet.
4. Sprinkle gilding flakes all over the sticky sheet and gently press them onto the sticky surface.
5. Shake the excess gilding flakes into a box for future use and carefully rub the remaining flakes so that they flatten and press into the surface of your project.
6. Cut round the shape of your peel-off, or cut a border to make a square or rectangular embellishment.

The gilding flakes will not stick to the black lines of your outline peel-off, giving a lovely metallic finish to the sections within the sticker.

Search 'gilding flakes' on YouTube for lots of great video tutorials on using this fabulous material.

Using outline stickers with glitter

To glitter the inside sections of an outline sticker, place it on a shape cut from a double-sided adhesive sheet. Use good-quality fine glitter and gently press down to make sure the glitter is as well stuck as possible.

If you choose complementary colours (such as pink, lilac and purple) you can use a teaspoon to sprinkle the glitters over different parts of the sticker. Because the colours work together, it doesn't matter if they run into each other. If, however, you want each section of your outline sticker to have its own distinct colour, there are various techniques you can use:

- Attach your outline sticker to white card and carefully use glitter glue to fill in the different sections. Tim Holtz Stickles is a good-quality glitter glue – and the bottles have a fine nozzle so that you can apply the glitter with precision.
- Fill in the sections with a glue pen and sprinkle on the glitter. Glue and glitter each section before moving on to the next.
- For a great tutorial on using the inset sections of the outline sticker as a mask, search for 'Glitter masking with outline stickers' on YouTube. Although a little time-consuming, this technique gives you the neatest possible finish.

For more on glitter and how to use it, see chapter 8.

Masking with chalk or ink

Outline stickers can be turned into quick and easy-to-use stencils. Simply press the sticker against a sleeve to make it a little less sticky, and place onto card. Dab over with chalk or an ink pad and carefully remove the sticker stencil to reveal the design.

Paper punches

Paper punches work on the same principle as the traditional round hole punch. They are hand-held, and they contain a shaped die that punches out a shape when you press down on the cutting mechanism.

About paper punches

The majority of punches are operated by pushing a button, but you can also get punches with levers and punches shaped like pliers.

'The majority of punches are operated by pushing a button, but you can also get punches with levers and punches shaped like pliers.'

Most punches only reach a short way in from the edge of the paper (not a good choice if you want to cut apertures in the middle of a large sheet of card). However, you can get long-reach punches which are shaped a bit like a stapler, and Martha Stewart Crafts also do a Punch All Over the Page (PAOP) range of punches. With the PAOP punch, the cutting mechanism is set into a small table-like frame, enabling you to place it wherever you want before pressing down to cut out your shape.

Paper punches also come in different sizes, ranging from mini punches that produce shapes of less than 1cm across to large punches that cut out shapes of 9 or 10cm. Woodware do a range of good-quality large punches in what they term jumbo, big, super, super duper and whopping sizes. The majority of punches only cut paper or lightweight card, although you should be able to use heavier card in the larger punches.

Different shapes, motifs and designs

Paper punches come in a huge variety of shapes, patterns and motifs:

Geometric shapes

It's useful to be able to make geometric shapes such as circles, squares, rectangles, diamonds, ovals and triangles. Circles are particularly handy for all sorts of effects, and it's well worth building up a collection of different sized circle punches. Large geometric punches are good for creating shapes for matting and layering (see chapter 10) and apertures for techniques such as iris folding (see chapter 1).

Motifs

There is a huge range of motifs to choose from, including flowers, leaves, hearts, teardrops, stars, snowflakes, butterflies, dragonflies, cats, dogs, balloons, candles, cakes, Christmas trees, eggs, hand prints, paw prints, teddies – to mention but a few!

Border punches

Border punches are used along the edge of the paper to create a shaped border. The punch is designed so that you can line up the notches with the punched holes, enabling you to punch whatever length of border you choose.

Corner punches

Corner punches cut a lacy pattern into the corner of a paper or card rectangle. You can also get punches that take the point off the corner to give it a rounded finish.

Punch and emboss punches

Punch and emboss punches both cut out a shape and indent it with an embossed pattern:

- Fiskars do a clever 4-in-1 Embossing Corner Punch that gives you four different corner punch patterns within the one punch, as well as adding embossed detail to the corner.
- X Cut do a Dimension Embossing Punch that punches out shapes such as flowers, leaves and butterflies – and adds an embossed pattern to the body of the shape.
- Martha Stewart Crafts do cute elephant and owl punches that also emboss details such as the owl's eyes and the elephant's ears.

Stationery punches

Punches that cut out labels, tags and envelope shapes are very useful. Woodware do a tag punch, and also a punch that cuts out a shape to fold into an envelope. A mini envelope makes an unusual embellishment for your card, particularly if you slip a special message inside. You can also get punches that produce postage stamp shapes with perforated edges.

Silhouette punches

With the exception of border and some corner punches, most paper punches cut out a single, solid shape. The Woodware Silhouette range is a little different in that it punches out small details within the main shape to create a much more intricate pattern. The collection includes buttons, butterflies, flowers and hearts – and some punches in the Silhouette range emboss the shape as well as punch it out.

'Punches that cut out labels, tags and envelope shapes are very useful.'

Multi-Shaper punches

The X Cut Multi-Shaper punch is a clever idea and very versatile. It can be used to punch different sized circles, ovals, squares and borders with a lacy edge. It's not the easiest tool to use and you need quite a strong pressure – but once you have mastered the technique, it's a useful product for making feminine cards. A die cutting machine produces similar results with much greater ease. However, die cutting machines are a lot more expensive than punches, and you also have to purchase a separate die for each shape. For more information about die cutting machines, see page 86.

Nesting punches

Nesting punches produce shapes that can be nested or layered, with each punch cutting out the same shape in a different size. A flower motif is a popular shape for a set of nesting punches. For ideas on layering punched flower shapes, see the next page.

Combination punches

Combination punches punch out a collection of single shapes that can be put together to create a complex image. Woodware do a small range of floral combination punches, including an iris, a violet and an orchid. If you punch shapes from different colours, you can mix them up to create a range of flowers with a matching colour scheme.

Threading and buckle punches

A threading punch cuts rows of small slots into card. This makes an easy way of threading ribbon, raffia or yarn along your card front. Buckle punches punch out a round or square buckle shape to decorate and thread with ribbon.

Using paper punches

There are lots of different ways to use a paper punch:

Layering flowers

If you have a collection of flower head punches in different sizes, you can layer them to create an endless variety of floral motifs for your cards. Try the following:

- Cover a small punched daisy in tacky PVA glue, press into silver micro-fine glitter and stick on top of a larger daisy head punched from pale blue pearlescent card. Scrape glitter from the centre of the flower and add a self-adhesive white pearl (adhesives often won't work on glitter, which is why you need to remove it before adding the pearl). Stick the layered flower onto a brilliant white card background.
- Use the same technique as above, but try combining gold glitter and pink pearlescent card with a cream or pink pearl centre on an ivory or cream card background.
- Punch lots of mini daisy shapes from good-quality white paper and lots of small circles from bright yellow paper. Layer two daisy shapes together and finish with a yellow centre to make beautiful and very realistic-looking daisies.

- Try layering different shaped flower heads, such as the Woodware 1cm mini daisy on top of the medium sized 2cm plum flower.

If you want to further explore making flowers from punched shapes, there's an excellent book available called *Paper Bouquet: Using Paper Punches to Create Beautiful Flowers* by Susan Tierney Cockburn. As an American publication, it can be hard to get hold of the punches you need – but most of them can be substituted with punches available in the UK. Joanna Sheen sells the book on her site (www.joannasheen.co.uk) and also stocks a limited range of the punches.

Punch art

'Punch art involves creating new images by arranging punched shapes.'

Punch art involves creating new images by arranging punched shapes. For example, teardrop shapes can be overlapped to make the petals of a flower. Hearts can be put together to make a four-leaf clover. Circles can be used to make a pram for a 'new baby' card: cut a large punched circle in half and a second circle into quarters, stick the quarter circle on the half circle to make the body of the pram and add two smaller circles for the wheels.

It is possible to create some really ingenious images with just a few simple shapes. If you want to try punch art for your cards and need inspiration, do an Internet images search for punch art and also see the book list.

Using the negative

With paper punching, you can use both the punched shape and the shaped hole that is left behind. The hole can be backed with coloured, patterned, textured or glittered card or paper. Try punching a row of shaped holes and sticking a strip of contrasting coloured paper behind to make a border pattern.

> **Try this – a gingham daisy**
>
> Punch a medium-sized daisy shaped hole into a piece of cream hammer card. Measure and cut around the daisy so that it is centred within a small square of card, and stick a strip of wide red gingham ribbon behind the hole so that it shows through. Mat and layer (see chapter 10) the daisy square onto a square torn from speckled handmade paper, a second square of cream hammer card and a square of hessian. Attach to a square card blank and stick tiny punched dots of gold mirri card around the hessian. Finish off the card by sticking a gold coloured flat-back jewel in the centre of the gingham flower.

Embossed effect background paper

Make an embossed effect background by punching lots of shapes and sticking them on a sheet of identical paper to create a subtle raised pattern. Give the background a more natural look by overlapping the edge of the paper with some of the shapes, and trimming them flush with the edge. This technique works well with simple shapes such as circles, hearts or stars and textured paper such as Bazzill Basics.

'If your punch starts cutting raggedy edges, sharpen it by punching a few times through sandpaper or silver foil.'

Punching problems

Occasionally, you will find that your paper punch plays up. Try the following troubleshooting techniques to deal with a punch that is blunt, sticky or jammed.

- Oily marks – New punches sometimes leave oily marks on the paper. Punch a few rough shapes to get rid of the manufacturer's oil.
- Blunt punch – If your punch starts cutting raggedy edges, sharpen it by punching a few times through sandpaper or silver foil.
- Stuck punch – If a button punch gets stuck, tap it sharply on a hard surface to release the mechanism. You can also try putting it in the freezer for a

while; as the cold makes the metal contract, it should release the punch. Bear in mind that your punch may be stuck because you are trying to cut too thick a card.

- Jammed punch – Some papers, such as fibrous mulberry, will jam a punch. Taking the greatest of care not to skewer yourself, try removing the wisps of paper with a pokey tool. If you can get all the pieces out, this should un-jam the punch.

Die cutting machines

A die cutting machine is a considered purchase because both the machine itself and the dies are expensive. If, however, you have the cash to invest in a die cutting machine, it will make a very useful addition to your craft cupboard.

The dies (the cutting shapes) are purchased separately from the machine, and die cutting enthusiasts gradually build up a large collection. A die cutting machine basically does the same as a paper punch – but it is much easier to use, offers a much wider selection of large shapes and is able to cut out far more intricate and detailed shapes. Die cutting machines can also emboss (see chapter 6).

Some die cutting machines are manual, some are electronic and some are computerised. Some will take different makes of die and embossing plate, whereas others only work with their own brand. Before deciding which to buy, investigate the various options. Online crafting forums are a good source of information, with experienced crafters giving their thoughts on the different brands – and if you join a forum, you can start your own thread asking for advice. The reviews on Amazon are also useful, particularly the American site (amazon.com) which tends to have a greater number.

Summing Up

- There are many different types of peel-off and sticker, although the outline sticker is the most versatile.
- Outline stickers can be coloured in, stuck onto background paper and cut out or glittered. They also make good stencils to use with chalks or inks.
- Most outline stickers are silver or gold, although they come in many other colours and finishes – including black and white, glitter, holographic, pearlescent and transparent, double-sided adhesive stickers.
- As well as shapes, motifs and images, you can also get Celtic, art deco and ornate patterns, medallions, embroidery peel-offs, corners and borders, sentiments, letters and numbers.
- Paper punches punch out shapes and motifs. You can also get border and corner punches, embossing punches and shape cutters to make doily-like circles and ovals.
- Punched shapes can be layered or arranged to make patterns or punch art images. The punched hole can also be backed with different coloured, textured and patterned paper, card or ribbon to create an attractive embellishment for your cards.

Chapter Six

Embossing and Stencilling

Embossing is a versatile paper decorating technique. Although embossing is simple to do, it results in an elegant and professional look – as long as you follow a few basic rules.

There are two main types of embossing: dry embossing and heat embossing. Both techniques produce a raised effect on the background card, although the actual techniques themselves are quite different.

Stencilling shares some similarities with dry embossing, except that you use a colouring medium to create the pattern rather than an embossing tool. Stencils can be used for both dry embossing and stencilling.

'Embossing is a versatile paper decorating technique.'

Dry embossing

The technique of dry embossing involves indenting a design in card stock with a stylus (embossing tool) to create a raised pattern. You will need the following equipment for your dry embossing project:

Brass or plastic stencils

A stencil is a thin sheet of brass or plastic, with cut-out shapes forming a motif, picture or pattern. Stencils can be simple or detailed, and they include images, letters, words, frames, borders, corners and backgrounds such as a dotty pattern.

Many stencils can be used in a die cutting and embossing machine, such as a Cuttlebug.

Embossing boards

Embossing boards are made from sturdy plastic. They are engraved with deep grooves in different shapes and patterns and they often come with their own scoring or embossing tool. Embossing boards are more likely to have borders, frames and tags than stencils, although you can also get embossing boards with images and motifs. The Glitter Girls (www.theglittergirls.co.uk) and Crafter's Companion (www.crafterscompanion.co.uk) both do a good range of embossing boards.

Embossing tools

'Although a light box is not essential, it is well worth getting one if you plan to do a lot of dry embossing.'

An embossing tool is a stylus with a handle (usually wooden) and a ball-shaped metal tip at each end. Embossing tools often come in packs of three with different sized metal balls, giving you a choice of tool for embossing small details or larger areas.

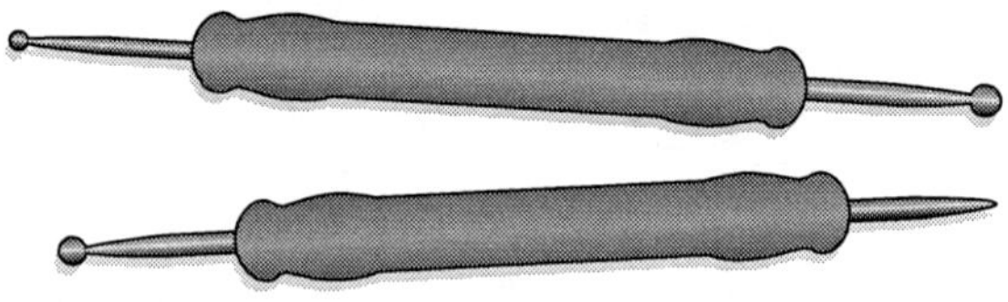

Light box

A light box is an opaque white plastic box containing a light bulb. Embossing on the light box illuminates the stencil and the card so you can see what you are doing. Although a light box is not essential, it is well worth getting one if you plan to do a lot of dry embossing. As an alternative, you can work on a glass table top with a table lamp underneath, or tape your stencil to a windowpane.

Low-tack tape

Tape is needed to fix the stencil to the light box and the card to the stencil, to make sure nothing slips while you are working. The tape must be low-tack so that it doesn't tear the card when you remove it. Scotch Magic Tape works well, or you can press regular masking tape against your sleeve a few times to reduce its stickiness.

Waxed paper, tumble dryer sheet or white candle

Rubbing waxed paper or a tumble dryer sheet across the card helps the embossing tool to move smoothly across the surface. Some crafters brush a little talcum powder or cornflour over the card. As an alternative, you can rub the tip of the embossing tool against a white candle. Experiment to find out which technique works best for you.

Lightweight card or sturdy paper?

If the paper is too thin, the embossing tool will tear into it. If the card is too thick, the impression won't show through on the other side. Go for a lightweight card or sturdy paper, and do a try-out first to check that your card or paper is suitable for embossing. Although you can, within reason, emboss on any card or paper finish, a pearlescent card gives a particularly effective result as it highlights the relief pattern. Embossed pearlescent also gives your card an elegant, sophisticated look.

How to dry emboss

In order to dry emboss, follow these steps:

1. Switch on your light box.
2. Tape your stencil onto the light box, making sure it is face downwards. This is particularly important if you are embossing letters or words.
3. Rub wax paper or a tumble dryer sheet over your embossing card.

4. Tape the card over the stencil. If the card is not double-sided, make sure the coloured surface is facing downwards.
5. Using an embossing tool, trace round the inside of each shape. You will need to exert some pressure to make sure the embossing tool creates an indentation. If you want to make the impression deeper, retrace the outlines.
6. When you have finished the design, remove the tape and turn the card over to admire the beautiful raised outline you have just created!

Some more tips:

- Use larger tools for big shapes and smaller tools for shapes where you have to work within a tight space.
- A finer tool is more likely to tear the card, so choose the largest ball nib that works for your purpose.
- Use a lighter touch with a thinner tool, and also with paper or thinner card.
- You do not need to emboss the area within the shape; embossing just the outline is sufficient to create the raised pattern on the other side of the card. Vellum is an exception to this rule, as embossing vellum creates a different effect from other papers – see page 94.
- It's hard to see where you are embossing on dark coloured card or paper, even on a light box. Start off with pale colours; only progress to darker colours when you know what you are doing, as you will have to rely on feeling the outlines of the stencil.

Embossing with an embossing board

Embossing with an embossing board is similar in principle to embossing with stencils. Tape your card face downwards on the board, and trace the indented lines with an embossing tool. As with stencil embossing, you will need to use wax paper, a tumble dryer sheet or a candle to help the tool move smoothly over the card.

Embossing with a board is quicker and easier to set up than a stencil. However, you are more likely to accidentally slip outside the groove. Going carefully will help to prevent this from happening – but if you do make a mistake, turn the card over and gently rub across the unwanted raised line to press it back down.

Not being able to see where you are going is the other disadvantage of an embossing board – and embossing boards usually include more than one image, which can add to the confusion. Always emboss the outer lines of the shape first as this prevents you from accidentally combining two shapes. You can also lift the card to check where you have got to, as long as you replace it in exactly the same position.

Die cutting and embossing machines

Die cutting machines can also be used for embossing (see chapter 5 for more on die cutting machines). The embossing templates for die cutting machines are called embossing folders. It's much easier to emboss with a machine than by hand as you simply place your card in the folder and run it through the machine. There are lots of different folders to choose from – and most folders will fit most machines, even though they are made by different companies.

'Embossing with a board is quicker and easier to set up than a stencil.'

Colouring a dry embossed pattern

You can leave your embossed pattern plain for a subtle effect, or you can add colour to bring out the design:

Colouring with chalks

Dusting your embossed pattern with chalk adds a delicious blush of colour. It's easier to get the chalk in the right place if you put the stencil back over the embossing. Simply apply the chalk to the visible sections, building it up in layers if you want a more intense colour. This technique looks best on white or pastel coloured card. For more on using chalks, see chapter 8.

Colouring with ink pads

Gently brush an ink pad over the raised parts of the embossing to add colour. This technique needs a light touch and an ink pad that isn't too 'juicy' or strongly coloured. Experiment with the different ink pads in your collection, to see which work best for this technique.

Colouring with other media

Chalks are generally regarded as the most effective way of colouring a dry embossed pattern, but you can use other colouring techniques:

'Embossing on vellum results in a beautiful effect as the embossing tool stretches the vellum and transforms it from translucent to opaque.'

- For a stronger colour, use pens – but bear in mind that the embossing technique stretches the fibres of the card, and this may cause the pens to bleed.
- Use water colour pencils to add colour to your embossed pattern. You can brush with a little water, but be careful not to soak the card as it will warp and cause wrinkles.
- Place the stencil over your pattern and brush the raised sections with mica powders mixed with a little water. As with water colour pencils, keep the water to a minimum to avoid wrinkles.

Dry embossing – some more techniques

There are a number of different effects you can create with the dry embossing technique.

Embossing on vellum

Embossing on vellum results in a beautiful effect as the embossing tool stretches the vellum and transforms it from translucent to opaque. Embossing on white vellum is perfect for wedding cards, new baby cards – and any other kind of cards where you want a dainty effect.

You can emboss just the outlines as usual. However, with vellum it's also worth embossing the inner part of the shapes. Because embossing changes the vellum from translucent to opaque, going over the whole shape has the effect of colouring in the design.

Try this – making a frosted flower

Stamp a flower with black ink onto scrap paper, place it on a soft surface such as the spongy side of a mouse mat, place vellum on top of the stamped image and trace the lines with the embossing tool. Cut out the flower and mount it on jewel coloured card to show off the frosted effect of the white embossed vellum.

Pergamano parchment craft

As you explore different card-making techniques, you will probably come across Pergamano or parchment craft. Although Pergamano is actually a brand name for tools and equipment, it's often used to describe the craft itself.

Dry embossing vellum could be described as a simple form of Pergamano. However, as well as embossing, Pergamano involves piercing, cutting, punching and tinting to create complex and beautiful lace-like patterns. Pergamano parchment is also heavier than vellum, and its translucent pale grey surface turns a startling white when embossed. If you want to try Pergamano, look out for classes or buy a good book (see the book list). For more information about Pergamano, visit www.artofparchmentcraft.com.

'Pergamano involves piercing, cutting, punching and tinting to create complex and beautiful lace-like patterns.'

Embossing on Core'dinations paper

Dry emboss a design on Core'dinations paper and gently sand over the raised pattern to reveal the colour core. For more on sanding with Core'dinations, see chapter 3.

Making backgrounds

Many embossing stencils are designed for making backgrounds. Background stencils have a repeating pattern of small motifs such as dots, flowers, butterflies, hearts, swirls and flourishes. They also come with patterns such as lines, checks, basket weave, honeycomb and lattice. It takes time and patience to hand emboss a background pattern, particularly if you want a large piece. A die cutting and embossing machine with a background template folder is much quicker and easier – although either technique will give you a beautiful texture to add to your card.

Making a shaped and embossed edge

An embossing board is a great way to make an embossed and shaped edge on a piece of card. Start off by embossing a patterned line on your card. Move the card forward and emboss an identical line, making sure there is a gap of a few millimetres between the two lines. Cut around the outer line to create a shaped edge, leaving the embossed inner line to mirror the shape of the edge.

Try this – embossing an envelope

Dry embossing is an easy way of decorating an envelope. For a special card, emboss an envelope made from pearlescent paper.

Cutting out embossed designs

A cut-out embossed image makes a lovely embellishment for a card. Choose a motif such as a heart, flower or butterfly, cut round the outer edge of the embossed outline and mount on foam pads to give a 3D effect.

Adding accents to embossed shapes

Some embossed motifs cry out for an added accent or embellishment. A flat-backed pearl, jewel or mother-of-pearl button makes a pretty centre for a flower embossed on pearlescent card. Add an organza bow with a dangly charm to an embossed heart, or a splash of glitter to the wings of an embossed butterfly. For more on these and other embellishments, see chapter 7.

> **Try this – monochrome effects**
>
> A single colour card can look very effective – and embossing is a great technique for adding visual interest without introducing a second colour. Try creating a white card with a pearly white embossed background and embellishments such as a white vellum flower (made with a silver outline sticker), white ribbon and white flat-backed pearls.

About heat embossing

Heat embossing is tremendous fun. Other than producing a raised line, it is a completely different technique from dry embossing. Heat embossing involves sprinkling embossing powder onto an inked image and heating the powder with a heat gun. The embossing powder is thermographic – which means that it melts when heated to produce a raised effect. Turning a dull, powdered image into a gleaming metallic relief design is one of the most magical techniques in card making!

'Turning a dull, powdered image into a gleaming metallic relief design is one of the most magical techniques in card making!'

Embossing ink pads and stamps

The standard technique for heat embossing is to stamp an image using a suitable ink pad, and sprinkle the image with embossing powder. The ink pad must be slow drying so that the powder will stick. Avoid using a finely detailed stamp; the powder expands when it is heated and the lines merge together if they are too close to each other. A fine embossing powder enables you to work with more detailed stamps than a regular grade (see overleaf). For more about stamps and embossing ink pads, see chapter 4

Embossing pens

An embossing ink pen is a useful tool if you want to create your own designs. Simply draw your image with the pen and sprinkle with embossing powder. Embossing pens are usually dual tipped, with a thin nib at one end for fine detail and a thick nib at the other for covering larger areas. The wonderful Sakura Quickie glue pen will also work for heat embossing.

Embossing powder

Embossing powder is sold in small tubs, and you can buy it in a range of different colours, thicknesses and finishes:

Regular, fine and coarse

Like coffee grounds, embossing powder comes in different grades. Unless marked otherwise, assume that an embossing powder is regular grade. A powder marked 'fine', 'super fine' or 'detail' gives a cleaner, sharper image and is good for more detailed stamps. Coarse grade gives a thicker, deeper cover and is used for large areas rather than fine detail (see UTEE on the following page).

For most projects, regular grade powder is the most suitable. Although you can use fine grade for any embossing, it has a tendency to leave a dusting of powder across the card (see page 102 for suggestions on how to deal with this).

Different colours

Embossing powder comes in just about every imaginable colour and shade, including pastels, brights, primary colours, earthtones, black and white, gold and silver. Although every card maker will have their favourite colours, white, black, gold and silver make a good starting point for the beginner. Even though the pots are quite small, a little goes a long way. If you have a crafting friend, consider sharing a pot so that you can gather a collection of colours for half the price.

Combining different coloured ink pads and embossing powders can affect the colour of your embossed image. A light coloured ink won't change the colour of a dark powder, but a light powder (such as white) on top of a strongly coloured ink (such as red) will lighten the colour of the ink to produce a milky pastel effect.

Clear embossing powder

A clear powder is another useful addition to your collection. When heated, it turns into a glassy, transparent raised layer. If you use it with a coloured ink pad, the colour shows through. If you use it with a clear embossing ink pad, the colour of the background card shows through. It can also be used with different coloured ink pads to create a glossy rainbow effect, or mixed with Perfect Peals mica powder for a shimmery effect.

'Combining different coloured ink pads and embossing powders can affect the colour of your embossed image.'

Different finishes

Apart from a wide range of colours, there are also lots of finishes to choose from. Try pearlescent, glitter, tinsel, metallic, fluorescent, transparent, opaque and puffy (when heated, puffy embossing powder fluffs up like marshmallow).

Tim Holtz Distress embossing powders

Tim Holtz's Distress embossing powders contain special release crystals. Shake the powder before use to make sure the crystals are evenly distributed. Once the powder has been heated, rub away the crystals to create a distressed, weathered look. The Distress embossing powders co-ordinate with Distress ink pads.

Ultra Thick Embossing Enamel (UTEE)

Like the Distress embossing powders, UTEE is made by the American company Ranger. It comes in the form of granules rather than powder. Used to cover larger areas, it looks like thick enamel once it has been heated. Although it can be melted with a heat gun, some UTEE projects require a piece of equipment called a melting pot. For more on using UTEE and melting pots, see page 106.

Heat guns

A heat gun is a bit like a small hairdryer, but with a more focused and intense heat. Make sure you buy one that is designed for crafting, rather than DIY.

A heat gun is pretty much a necessity if you want to heat emboss. It is possible to use other heating methods – such as holding the project over a toaster – but these techniques give somewhat haphazard results and can also be dangerous. A hairdryer will not work as it doesn't get hot enough and produces too strong an air current. It goes without saying that you need to use the heat gun with care; not only does it get very hot, it also takes a while to cool down. Heat guns are not suitable for children to use.

Embossing on card, paper and other surfaces

As long as a surface can withstand the blast of hot air from the heat gun, you can use it for heat embossing:

Glossy surfaces

Although you can't normally use a slow-drying ink on glossy card, this isn't a problem with heat embossing as the melted powder fixes the ink onto the glossy surface.

Card

Cardstock generally works better than paper as it is less prone to wrinkling or scorching. If you have problems with wrinkling, plan a design where you can emboss onto separate card and stick it to the card front – rather than working directly onto the card itself. The process of sticking, particularly with a dry adhesive such as double-sided tape, should straighten out the wrinkles. See page 102 for more suggestions on how to avoid wrinkles.

Mulberry paper

Mulberry makes a pretty background for embossing, but you do need to be very careful not to scorch the paper. If this is a problem, try embossing onto card-backed mulberry.

Vellum

Heat embossed vellum looks beautiful, but it requires special care as it will suddenly shrivel if it is overheated. Move the heat gun from area to area as quickly as possible – and be prepared for a few disasters while you are getting the hang of it! If you struggle with heat embossing vellum, try heating it from behind – underneath the stamped image. This makes it easier to see the second the powder melts so you can move on to the next bit straightaway.

Acetate

You can heat emboss onto acetate, as long as the acetate is the heat-resistant type designed for laser printers.

How to heat emboss

In order to heat emboss, follow these steps:

1. Stamp an image using a suitable stamp pad, or draw a design with an embossing pen.
2. Place the card on a heat-proof surface, such as a heat-resistant craft sheet – see below.
3. Sprinkle on the embossing powder. Cover the whole image with a thick layer of powder.
4. Pour the excess powder back into the pot.
5. Gently flick the back of the card to remove any particles that are sticking to the un-inked parts.
6. If necessary, use a small dry paint brush or cotton bud to wipe away excess powder.
7. Plug in your heat gun, switch it on and let it heat up.
8. Hold the heat gun several centimetres above the embossing powder until it melts and fuses to create a glossy, raised surface.

Heat-proof craft sheets

A heat-proof, non-stick craft sheet is an extremely handy piece of kit. You can use it for any activity that involves heat, and it's also good for wet activities such as spraying with mists or using alcohol inks. The craft sheet looks a bit like sturdy brown paper with a smooth, non-stick finish. Many craft stores and websites stock the sheets as part of their tools and equipment range.

Tips and troubleshooting

- If the embossing powder sticks to the un-inked parts of the card, and you can't get it off with a paint brush or cotton bud, rub over the card with an anti-static pad before you start (try the Magic Anti-Static Bag). You can also use a tumble dryer sheet, talcum powder or make your own bag by putting cornflour into a baby's sock.
- Some crafters like to put a coffee filter paper under their work (the ones shaped like cupcake cases, not the flat cones). The cup shape catches the powder and can be folded into a chute for pouring the powder back into the pot.
- If the heat gun scorches or wrinkles the card, try the following:

1. Hold the heat gun further away from the card surface and move it on the moment the powder melts.
2. Move the heat gun gently from side to side rather than keeping it still. This diffuses the heat a little and prevents one area from getting too hot.
3. Make sure your heat gun is hot enough. A properly heated gun will melt the powder swiftly, enabling you to move on to the next bit before the card scorches or wrinkles.
4. Try embossing on a wire cake rack, as this will help the card to cool more quickly.
5. Try heating the back of the card.
6. Using long tweezers, hold a small shape in the air when you heat it.

- If the embossed line is dull and flat, you may be overheating the powder – see above.
- If your embossed line is flat and thin, you may need more powder. Make sure your ink pad is juicy enough (older ink pads can get too dry) and check that you are not leaving the ink too long before sprinkling on the powder. Take the lid off the powder and have everything ready so you can sprinkle it on as soon as you have inked the card.
- If the powder stays granular and flakes off the card, you haven't heated it for long enough. Make sure your heat gun is hot enough and that you are holding it over the powder for a sufficient length of time.

Heat embossing – some more techniques

Apart from straightforward heat embossing with stamped images, there are some other techniques you can try:

Embossing resist

Heat embossed lines and areas are waterproof and will resist water-based colour such as mica powders mixed with water, Cosmic Shimmer Mists or dye-based inks. Heat emboss your design and then brush or spray across the card with your chosen colour medium.

A piece of sponge or an ink blending tool is the easiest way to apply inks. For a light, watery ink effect, follow these steps:

- Dab the dye-based ink pad onto a non-stick craft sheet.
- Spritz with a water spray bottle to dilute the ink.
- Pick up the spritzed ink from the craft sheet with a blending tool or sponge.
- Dab over the embossed image.

If there are any beads of colour left on the embossed lines, carefully wipe them away with a cotton bud.

Choose colours that have a good contrast. For example, if you want to dab orange and yellow ink over a red embossed image, make sure the red embossing powder is a strong shade that will stand out. White embossing powder is effective against darker colours, and clear powder will show up as the colour of the background card.

Heat embossing over chalk

Dab chalk over card to create a colourful misty pattern (see chapter 8 for information on using chalks). Spray with fixative, making sure that every part is covered. Once the fixative is bone dry, stamp and emboss your design. Black embossing powder shows up well against the soft colours of the chalk, but you can experiment with whatever colour combinations you wish.

Colouring an embossed image

If you emboss a stamped image with black embossing powder, the raised black lines make it easier to colour in the image with pens, mica powders, glitter or water colours. The intense black lines also look good against the colours, particularly the shimmery tones of mica powder or Sakura gel pens.

Embossed scribble pattern

Using the thin nib of an embossing pen, lightly scribble over card with loose curves and loops. Randomly stud the scribble with dots made by the thick nib, sprinkle with gold or silver powder and emboss. The random pattern makes an effective decoration for hearts, stars or panels.

Embossing shapes

Punch a shape from heat resistant double-sided adhesive sheet. Sprinkle with embossing powder and heat to create a sticky-backed embossed shape.

Embossing strips

Place a strip of double-sided tape along your card – preferably the heat-resistant red kind. Remove the protective paper, cover the sticky tape with embossing powder and heat to create an embossed border. Experiment with different widths of tape. You can also create an embossed border using low-tack tape. Place two strips of tape on your card, with a gap in-between. Press an embossing ink pad over the tape so that the gap is covered with a layer of ink. Remove the tape, sprinkle on embossing powder and heat.

Embossing with UTEE

The thicker texture of UTEE enables you to create some impressive effects:

Triple embossing

You will need a chipboard or Grungeboard shape for this technique (see chapter 3). Using sponge or a blending tool, cover the shape with ink and add a stamped pattern if you wish. Press the shape into a Versamark ink pad and cover with clear UTEE powder. Heat until melted, sprinkle with a second coat of UTEE and heat again. Repeat the process a third time to give a thick glassy coating. If a coat cools before you manage to sprinkle on the next layer of granules, simply reheat the UTEE to melt it again.

'The thicker texture of UTEE enables you to create some impressive effects.'

Triple embossing paper shapes

A shape punched from sturdy patterned paper can be triple embossed with clear UTEE. Flowers, butterflies, hearts and stars all work well – and the butterfly's wings can be folded upwards before the UTEE dries to create a 3D effect. Hold the shape with tweezers to make sure your fingers don't get burnt.

Stamping into UTEE

Triple emboss a piece of sturdy card with UTEE. You can use clear powder over coloured card, or do a final layer using ordinary embossing powder to add a coloured surface. While the embossing powder is still hot, press in a rubber stamp (don't worry about damaging your stamp, the rubber will withstand the heat). Wait until the embossing powder has completely hardened before removing the stamp – at least a minute and possibly longer. You can use just the stamp to create an impression in the UTEE, or ink it to add a stronger line. Choose a stamp with a simple outline, and avoid stamps with too much detail.

UTEE and mica powders

Mix a mica powder such as Perfect Pearls with the dry UTEE to create a shimmery, pearly finish. Apply areas of different coloured UTEE for a marbled rainbow effect. You can also sprinkle dry mica powder onto the UTEE while it is still hot.

UTEE and glitter

Sprinkle glitter onto UTEE while still hot, or sprinkle glitter onto the UTEE before heating. You can also sprinkle on accent beads (see chapter 7) or embed items such as charms, buttons or beads.

Cracking UTEE

Put your UTEE embossed project in the freezer for about 10 minutes. When you take it out, gently bend the card to crack the UTEE. This gives an aged, 'cracked glass' look. You can add to the distressed effect by rubbing ink into the cracks with a blending tool or sponge.

Using a Ranger Melting Pot

A Ranger Melting Pot is a non-stick vessel that can be used for melting UTEE, among other crafting media. Once the UTEE is melted, you can stir in Ranger Melt Art Heat It inks to create marbled effects, and cover shapes by dipping them into the molten enamel. You can also pour the molten UTEE onto a heat-proof craft sheet and stamp into it, or pour it into small moulds to make embellishments (Ranger does a product for making your own moulds, called Mold-N-Pour). If you would like to see a demo of the Melting Pot, American designer Suze Weinberg has recorded a YouTube tutorial called 'Ranger Melting Pot Basics'.

Take care . . .

Be very careful with the molten UTEE as it gets extremely hot. When dipping a shape or heating it, use long tweezers and watch that the enamel doesn't drip onto your fingers.

Stencilling

Like dry embossing, stencilling uses templates with cut-out shapes. The difference is that you create the pattern by adding colour, rather than using an embossing tool.

Using a stencil

Use low-tack tape to attach the stencil to card and apply whichever colour medium you have chosen to use. The stencil masks areas of the card so that the colour only takes on the cut-out sections. When you have finished, remove the stencil to reveal the coloured design. The following colour media work well with stencils:

'The stencil masks areas of the card so that the colour only takes on the cut-out sections.'

Chalks

Using the sponge applicator that comes with the chalks, brush colour over the cut-out parts of the stencil. Add the chalk little by little to build colour intensity. Once the stencil has been removed, spray with fixative so the chalk doesn't smudge.

Sprays

There is a wide range of beautiful spray media available, and they work particularly well for stencilling. Mist across the stencil, rather than directly at it. For more on sprays, see chapter 8.

Inks

Apply inks in a similar way to chalks. Use a sponge applicator and pick up the colour from an ink pad, or apply alcohol inks using a blending tool.

Embossing paste

This thick paste is specially designed to be used with stencils, and it comes in various colours including white, gold and silver. To stencil with embossing paste, follow these steps:

- Tape the stencil to card with low tack tape.
- Using a palette knife, take a thick blob of paste.
- Scrape the palette knife across the stencil to apply the paste (a bit like buttering bread).
- Scape back over the stencil with the knife to remove the excess.
- If you have missed a bit, you can go over it again – but keep the number of applications to a minimum, as you will eventually push the paste under the stencil and smudge the image.
- When you have finished applying the paste, carefully lift the stencil from the bottom edge (as if the top edge were a hinge) to reveal the pattern.
- While the paste is still wet, you can sprinkle on glitter or mica powder.

Once dry, the paste creates a raised effect that can be coloured or tinted with ink, chalk or mica paint.

> **Washing the stencil**
>
> Embossing paste is very hard to remove once dry. Make sure you wash the stencil while the paste is still wet.

Summing Up

- Embossing involves creating a raised design. There are two different types of embossing – dry embossing and heat embossing.
- Dry embossing requires a stencil, light box and embossing tool. You can also use an embossing board or a die cutting and embossing machine. The embossed pattern can be left plain or coloured with chalks or inks.
- Heat embossing is a different process from dry embossing. It involves stamping an image with an embossing ink pad, sprinkling on embossing powder and heating with a heat gun to melt the powder and produce a glossy, raised effect.
- Embossing powder comes in a wide range of colours and finishes, including gold, silver clear, pearlescent and glittered. It also comes in different grades – regular for everyday use, fine for detailed embossing and coarse for creating a thick enamelled coating.
- An embossing pen can be used if you want to heat emboss your own patterns and images, and embossed patterns can also be used as a resist for water-based colours.

Chapter Seven

Some More Embellishments

So far, we have looked at making embellishments using the key techniques of stamping, paper punches and peel-offs. In this chapter we explore the many other embellishments you can use on your cards.

'Gems, pearls and buttons are extremely useful for adding the perfect finishing touch to your cards.'

Gems, pearls and buttons

Gems, pearls and buttons are extremely useful for adding the perfect finishing touch to your cards.

Gems

There are lots of faceted flat-backed acrylic gems to choose from. They come in all colours and sizes, and although the majority are round, you can also get square, teardrop, heart, star and flower shapes. Some are self-adhesive and some need to be glued. A little spot of tacky glue or a strong sticky dot is the securest way to stick them – and a pokey tool (see chapter 2) is useful for removing a self-adhesive gem from its backing paper and manoeuvring it onto the card.

Gems make pretty little centres for punched or stamped flowers. They also create a sparkly finishing touch if you glue them in a row along the edge of the card. Adhesive gemstones come in the form of a design as well as singly – often a flourish, a star-shape or an initial. The design can be carefully lifted from the backing paper (a bit like a delicate peel-off) and placed on the card to make a fabulously blingy embellishment. See the help list for details of online sellers of gems and other embellishments.

Pearls

Flat-backed pearls are similar to gems, except that they are smooth pearlescent cabochons rather than clear faceted acrylic. You can get brightly coloured pearls, but the majority come in white, cream or pastel shades.

Pearls can be used in much the same way as gems. They create a more subtle look than gems, adding a soft gleam rather than a sparkle. They work particularly well with ribbon and pearlescent card.

Make your own pearls

Using a pearl glue, such as Cosmic Shimmer Pearl PVA, make your own flat-backed pearls for finishing off your cards. This works out much cheaper than buying them ready-made and, with a bit of practice, you can create something just as beautiful.

Using the waxed backing paper from an outline sticker sheet, carefully squeeze pearls of glue onto the sheet. Once they are completely dry, peel them off the sheet and stick them to your card with a glue pen or a dot of tacky PVA. Pearl glue comes in lots of different colours, or you can colour white pearls with an alcohol pen. You can also sprinkle on a little glitter while still wet to create a sparkly pearl.

Apart from the satisfaction of making your own pearls, you can use as many as you like on your cards without having to count the cost!

Buttons

Buttons are great for adding a homespun look to your card, and you can also thread thin ribbon, twine, string or raffia through the holes to create extra detail. Buttons can either be sewn onto the card front or stuck on with tacky glue.

Buttons have lots of uses. They make great centres for flowers and they can also be used to fill in a simple shape, such as a heart, or stuck round an outline. Larger buttons can be matted and layered and used as the focal point of a card (see chapter 10).

Buttons from haberdashers are expensive. You may want to choose a particularly large and decorative button as the main embellishment for a special card, but you can end up paying a pound or more. Buttons sold in packs for crafting purposes are much better value and you can also get patterned, translucent, glittered and shaped buttons. www.craftisland.co.uk has a fabulous selection to choose from. You can also save buttons from old clothes. Small mother-of-pearl buttons are particularly useful for floral or rustic style cards.

Ribbons, bows and other fibres

Ribbons, bows and lace are essential to card making – and there are many other fibres you can use, including hessian or jute ribbon, string, twine, embroidery silks, textured wool and raffia.

Ribbons

'Ribbon has an endless number of uses in card making, and it can be used in every style of card.'

Ribbon has an endless number of uses in card making, and it can be used in every style of card, from distressed and homespun to elegant and cute.

There are many different types of ribbon, including:

- Polyester satin – This is the standard ribbon, with a smooth satiny finish and woven edges. A useful, all-purpose ribbon,
- Organza – Organza is a filmy, transparent ribbon, and it doesn't fray when cut. It's great for pretty, girly cards, wedding cards and new baby cards.
- Grosgrain – Grosgrain is a robust ribbon with a horizontally ribbed texture. Grosgrain ribbon in masculine colours works well for men's cards.
- Lurex or lamé ribbon – Lurex or lamé ribbon is made from a stiff, metallic fabric. It usually comes in shiny gold or silver and adds a festive touch to Christmas cards.
- Velvet ribbon – This is ribbon with a velvet surface and rich colours. Perfect for giving your cards a luxurious finish.
- Picot-edged – Picot-edged ribbon is made from satin or organza with a pattern of small loops along the edges.
- Twill tape – Twill tape is a heavy woven cotton ribbon that looks good on rustic, homespun and distressed style cards.

- Hessian or jute ribbon – Hessian or jute ribbon is a wide, loosely woven ribbon that can be cut into squares and rectangles to make textured backgrounds. It works well with natural materials such as handmade papers.
- Lace ribbon – Lace can be purchased in a range of different widths and patterns. It's a useful embellishment for feminine cards – and it also has other uses in craft making.

Ribbon comes in various widths, ranging from 3mm to over 6cm, and it's usually sold by the metre. If you use a particular ribbon regularly, it's worth buying a whole spool as it will work out much cheaper in the long run.

Apart from different widths and finishes, you can also get a variety of patterns. Spots, stripes, tartans, little motifs woven into the ribbon and stitches down the centre or sides of the ribbon are all useful for adding detail to your cards. Gingham ribbon is particularly versatile. In reds and navy blues, it's perfect for the homespun look, and in pale pink and blue, it works well for new baby and Christening cards.

'You can buy ready-tied bows or you can make your own.'

Bows

You can buy ready-tied bows or you can make your own. To tie a bow, follow these steps:

1. Fold a length of ribbon to create two loops.
2. Cross the loops over and tie them together.
3. Adjust the loose ends and the loops to get them the right size, neaten the knot of the bow and pull the loops tight.

Using ribbons and bows in card making

The following are just a few ideas for using ribbons and bows:

- A simple ribbon border – Stick a length of ribbon down the edge of a card, or along the top and/or bottom. Add a bow and a few flat-backed pearls, gems or small buttons.
- A central ribbon – A length of ribbon stuck down the centre of the card and used as a background for motifs can look very effective.

- Ribbon and lace – Stick a length of lace along your card and add a length of narrower satin ribbon so that it runs either alongside or down the centre of the lace.
- An ornate ribbon border – Stick a length of polyester satin or velvet ribbon alongside a gold peel-off strip and a strip cut from patterned paper to create an ornate border. Make sure the ribbon, peel-off and paper strip are all different widths. This is even more effective if you shape the outer edge of the paper strip with fancy scissors.
- Covering a join – A length of ribbon makes a neat way of hiding the join between two contrasting mats.
- Hiding adhesive – Tying ribbon around the spine of a card covers the adhesive used to attach acetate or vellum.
- A ribbon wrap – Glue thin ribbon around a cut-out shape.
- Matting and layering ribbon – Stick a length of ribbon down the centre of a card strip. The card strip can either be left straight-edged, or shaped with fancy scissors or a border punch. Stick a length of thin ribbon on top of a length of thick ribbon, using contrasting colours. Stick a bow tied from the thin ribbon on top of a bow tied from the thick ribbon, and add to the layered ribbon lengths.
- Tying a gatefold card – Glue a length of thin polyester satin or wide organza ribbon to the back of a gatefold card. Tie the loose ends in a bow at the front of the card, to keep the two sides shut.

- Threading ribbon – Punch slots in your card with a threading punch (see chapter 5) and weave ribbon in and out of the card, securing the loose ends on the inside with sticky tape.
- Backing a punched shape – Stick patterned ribbon such as gingham, tartan or striped ribbon behind the shaped hole made by a paper punch.
- Adding a bow – Apart from adding a bow to any of the previously mentioned ribbon embellishments, there are many different ways of using bows to finish off a card:

'Robust ribbons such as grosgrain, twill tape and satin polyester are easy to stick with tacky PVA glue.'

Sticking ribbon

Sticking ribbon to card is not particularly tricky, but there are a few rules to bear in mind – and depending on the fabric they are made from, some ribbons require different types of adhesive.

The basics

Robust ribbons such as grosgrain, twill tape and satin polyester are easy to stick with tacky PVA glue. To stick a length of ribbon down or across a card front, follow these steps:

1. Using a ruler and pencil, make a guideline to show exactly where you want the ribbon to go. If you are using a white or pale ribbon, keep the pencil line as light as possible to prevent it from showing through.
2. Cut a length of ribbon at least four centimetres longer than the card.
3. Using a pokey tool, apply small dots of glue to the ribbon and rub it into a smooth layer. The layer needs to be as thin as possible, particularly with light coloured polyester satin.
4. Stretch the ribbon to keep it straight, and lay it on the card along the pencil guideline.
5. If you haven't got it positioned correctly on the first go, you can peel it off and try again – although the layer of glue will dry out if you make too many attempts.
6. Trim the overlapping ribbon with sharp scissors so the ends are flush with the edges of the card.

You can also use double-sided tape, or run the ribbon through a Xyron machine if you have one. A dry adhesive has the advantage of not soaking through the ribbon – and it also covers the whole surface so that the ribbon sticks down smoothly. On the downside, you only get one chance to position the ribbon exactly where you want it.

Sticking organza ribbon

Sticking organza ribbon presents similar challenges to sticking vellum or acetate, as the adhesive shows through. If possible, attach organza ribbon by threading it through eyelets or holes punched into the card. You can also use large glue dots or a dab of tacky glue to secure the ribbon at each end and under the bow. Cover the glued area with an embellishment if the adhesive shows through.

Sticking hessian ribbon

Sticking loosely woven hessian or jute ribbon is also challenging because of its loose weave. If you don't cover every strand with adhesive, the hessian won't lie flat. You get the most reliable results by using a pokey tool to apply tacky PVA to each strand – although this is time-consuming. You can also try a spray glue, but make sure it is strong enough to hold the weight of the hessian.

Preventing frayed ends

If you have cut ends on your cards, either on a bow or at the tips of a ribbon border, seal them with PVA glue to stop them from fraying. Using a pokey tool, spread a thin layer of glue along the cut edge and leave to dry clear. Organza ribbon shouldn't fray, so this treatment is only necessary for polyester satin and grosgrain ribbons.

Try this - colouring ribbon

White or pale coloured ribbon can be coloured using alcohol pens, rubbing the ribbon across a pigment-based ink pad or brushing with alcohol inks. You can also use a dye-based ink pad, although the colour tends not to be so vibrant. Pigment inked ribbon takes a while to dry; if you are in a hurry, speed up the process with a heat gun.

Satin, polyester, grosgrain and organza ribbons are all suitable for colouring. You can also colour clear flat-backed gems and pearls with alcohol pens, enabling you to create matching ribbons and jewels.

Other fibres

Other fibres such as string, raffia and textured wool can be used for winding around a cut-out shape, threading through punched slots or threading through the holes of a button.

An increasingly popular fibre from America is Baker's Twine. This is a thin, pale coloured string with patches of red, green or blue. If you find it hard to source in the UK, or want to save money, there's a clever YouTube video tutorial on how to make your own (search for 'Make your own Baker's Twine').

Brads, eyelets and charms

Brads, eyelets and charms are all metal embellishments. Brads and eyelets are both decorative and useful – and charms are a cute way to add a finishing touch to a special card.

Brads

Brad is another name for a paper fastener. Brads consist of two flat pointed stems attached to a decorative head. To use the brad, the stems are pushed through card and then split apart to fix the head to the other side of the card.

Brads come in lots of different shapes, sizes and colours, ranging from the classic gold stud to shaped and patterned motifs such as Christmas stockings, hearts and large coloured flowers. You can use a brad simply as an embellishment, or you can use it as a decorative way of attaching hard-to-stick papers such as vellum and acetate (see chapter 3).

Although the ends of the brad are pointed, they are not sharp enough to pierce the card without creasing it. Always make a little hole to start you off. The easiest way to do this is with a pokey tool or the tip of your craft knife.

'Brads and eyelets are both decorative and useful – and charms are a cute way to add a finishing touch to a special card.'

Eyelets

Eyelets are small metal rings that can be fixed onto a hole punched in card to create a reinforced lining. The eyelet consists of a metal ring attached to a small metal tube. To fix eyelets, you will need an eyelet setter, a hammer and a soft mat, such as an old computer mouse mat.

1. Punch or pierce a small hole in the card. Some eyelet setters include punches.
2. Place the eyelet upside down on the mat and place the card on top so that the tube at the back of the eyelet pokes through the hole.
3. Position the tip of your eyelet setter in the tube and bang it with a hammer until the tube splits and flattens around the edge of the hole.
4. Turn the card over to see how the metal ring is securely and neatly fixed around the hole in your card.

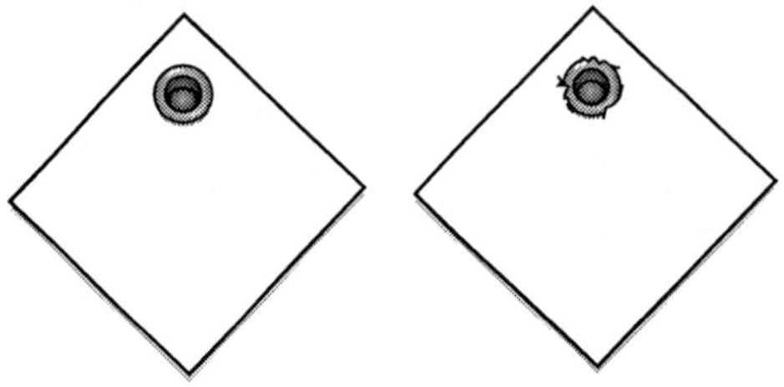

> **Spring-loaded eyelet setters and Crop-A-Diles**
>
> You can buy spring-loaded eyelet setters that don't need to be bashed with a hammer. They are more expensive, but quieter and easier to use. If you want to use eyelets on a regular basis, look into buying a We R Memory Keepers Crop-A-Dile. This is by far the simplest way to set eyelets and it also works on chipboard, wood, leather and many other materials.

Ideas for using brads and eyelets

- Put a brad at each corner of a square or rectangle, at the top and bottom of a die cut oval or at each end of a card strip. This is a decorative way of fixing the shapes to the card blank.
- Punch small coloured hearts from card and fix each one to the card blank with a brad. Choose contrasting colours, such as red hearts and yellow brads, or a mix of colours for a bright, cheerful effect.
- Put a row of coloured brads along a strip of card to make a studded border.
- Use both brads and eyelets as flower centres, use eyelets to make the portholes in a boat and small black or brown brads for an animal's eyes.
- Use an eyelet to decorate the hole in a tag or luggage label.
- Thread ribbon through a row of eyelets set into your card blank.

- Set an eyelet into the top of a die cut sentiment, punch a hole at the top of the card blank and tie the sentiment to the card using ribbon or Baker's Twine.
- Using a lattice patterned embossing board or folder (see chapter 6), emboss a piece of card and fix small brads to the points where the embossed lines cross.
- Use round and star shaped brads to decorate a Christmas tree and shiny red brads to make holly berries.
- Using silicone glue, stick flat-backed jewels or pearls onto the head of a brad.
- Colour the metal brads and eyelets with alcohol pens or alcohol inks.

Charms

Charms make a pretty addition to a card and you can get a wide variety of different motifs. They come in brass, silver tone or gold tone, and some are also coloured. They usually have a loop so that you can tie them to your card with ribbon. Depending on the quality of the charm, they can be quite expensive – but they do add a luxurious touch to special occasion cards such as weddings or Christenings.

'Charms make a pretty addition to a card and you can get a wide variety of different motifs.'

Ready-made toppers and embellishments

A ready-made embellishment or topper is a quick and easy way of making a card. Choices include:

- Die cut and decorated foam shapes.
- Die cut and decorated paper shapes, such as a wedding set with a bride's dress, groom's suit and top hat, wedding cake and bouquet.
- Flat wooden shapes, including animals and insects.
- Flat-backed motifs made from coloured Fimo modelling clay (you can also try making your own).
- Blossoms made from thick mulberry paper or fabric.

- Padded fabric motifs and shapes, such as hearts, stars, teddies and rabbits.
- Bunches of tiny fabric flowers.
- Wire and gauze sequinned butterflies.
- Printed images.

A small ready-made embellishment such as a fabric flower can be used as a finishing touch. Alternatively, you can use an embellishment as the focal point of the card. This can be very handy if you want to make a card for a specialised occasion such as a graduation. The illustration shows a graduation card with a ready-made topper cut from a black foam sheet, set against a matted and layered background.

eBay is a great place to buy card toppers and embellishments, both manufactured and handmade.

Decoupage, pyramage and invertage

Decoupage, pyramage and invertage are three related papercrafting techniques that can be used to make attractive dimensional embellishments for your cards.

About decoupage

Traditional decoupage is a Victorian craft that involves pasting cut-out images onto a surface and covering them with a clear glaze. In the card-making world, decoupage has come to mean building up an image in layers to create a three-dimensional effect.

When you first start out with decoupage, work with specially designed decoupage sheets. These are printed with a main image and a series of increasingly small details taken from the main image. To make things even easier, you can get pre-cut decoupage sheets – saving you from having to cut out the images yourself. To use the pre-cut sheets, simply pop out the shapes and trim off the little tabs if necessary. You can also get sheets where the images are numbered, to help you stick them on in the correct order.

To make your decoupage embellishment, follow these steps:

- Cut out the main image and stick it onto your card background using foam pads or silicon glue to add dimension.
- Cut out the next largest detail, and stick it over the matching part of the main image, again using foam pads or silicon glue.
- Continue cutting out details and building them up in layers, finishing off with the smallest detail.

The decoupage embellishment can be glazed and decorated with small bows, gems, pearls or glitter – just like any other image.

Some practical tips for making decoupage

- If the printed images are intricate, use small, sharp scissors or decoupage snips to cut them out (see chapter 2).

- For tips on cutting out with scissors, see chapter 2.
- Don't position the foam pads right on the edges of the shape, or they will show.
- Make sure the foam pads are not too far in as the edges of the shape can bend if they are completely unsupported.
- Colour white foam pads with alcohol pens to match the colour of your images.
- If you are decoupaging a lot of layers, use thin foam pads to avoid ending up with a skyscraper! As an alternative, use silicone glue as it allows you to create exactly the thickness you want.
- If you position an image in the wrong place, carefully slice through the foam with a sharp craft knife and re-stick it.
- Unlike foam pads, silicon glue enables you to gently move the image about until you have got it in exactly the right place.
- Make a boxelope for your decoupaged cards (see chapter 1).

'If you are decoupaging a lot of layers, use thin foam pads to avoid ending up with a skyscraper!'

Other sources of decoupage

Many crafting CDs include decoupage images that you can print out. You can also download free sheets from the Internet – try www.3dsheets.com or www.freecraftdownloads.co.uk. Free downloads enable you to practise your decoupage skills without having to make mistakes on sheets you have paid for.

Pyramage

Pyramage is similar to decoupage, except that it involves placing smaller and smaller pictures centrally on top of each other to create a pyramid shape (if you use square or rectangular pictures) or a cone shape (if you use round or oval pictures).

Invertage

Invertage uses the frames left over from pyramage. Start off by sticking the complete picture to the background card. Stick the frame with the smallest hole on top so that it fits exactly over the complete picture. Continue building up the invertage using frames with larger and larger holes – finishing with the largest. The end result creates an image with an inverted pyramid or an inverted cone.

Quilling

Quilling is an ancient craft that involves rolling thin strips of paper into intricate designs and gluing them onto a background. The rolled shapes are stuck end on to create a 3D effect (imagine the strips of paper as tiny hedges forming a maze).

To make the shapes, the end of the paper strip is inserted into a slotted tool and wound around the tip of the tool. By squeezing the coils of paper, different shapes can be created, including teardrops, crescent moons and leaves. For online information, go to the Paper Quilling section of www.handmade-craft-ideas.com.

'Quilling is an ancient craft that involves rolling thin strips of paper into intricate designs and gluing them onto a background.'

Angelina Fibres

Angelina Fibres is a fabulous resource that you can turn into a shimmering sheet material reminiscent of Angel Hair (see chapter 3). Angelina Fibres comes in a wide variety of colours, and you can also get different finishes such as metallic, pearl and holographic.

Angelina Fibres start out as a jumbled mass of iridescent threads. The fibres are made from heat-bondable shredded polyester film – which means that they melt and stick together when heated. To use the Angelina Fibres, tease them out to make the threads a little less tangled, place them between two sheets of baking parchment and iron over the parchment. The fibres will melt to form a thin, crisp, iridescent sheet which can be peeled off the parchment once it has cooled down.

Put the iron on a silk setting and adjust the heat if it's not hot enough to melt the fibres. When you first start out, make sure that you use the heat-bondable or Hot-Fix type of fibre, as non-heat-bondable fibres require the addition of a special bonding powder.

Even the heat-bondable fibres will only bond to themselves when they melt. This means that you cannot fuse the fibres onto card, fabric or other surfaces. If you want to bond the fibres to a surface, use a bonding powder such as Super Mend Bonding Powder (available from www.rainbowsilks.co.uk, which also sell the fibres and different sized ironing sheets).

There is so much you can do with Angelina Fibres. The following are just a few of the many possibilities:

- Mixing colours – Mix coloured fibres before ironing to make a multicoloured sheet.
- Making shapes – Cut the Angelina sheet into shapes.
- Moulding shapes – Run the iron over cut-out shapes and mould them while still warm and pliable (taking great care not to burn your fingers!) Try curling a butterfly's wings, a leaf or the petals of a flower to create a 3D embellishment.
- Stamping with inks – Stamp with inks onto an Angelina sheet.
- Making indented impressions – Place a layer of fibres over a simple, bold rubber stamp, lay baking parchment on top and press down with the iron to melt the fibres. The rubber stamp leaves an impression in the Angelina sheet and will peel off easily once the sheet is cool.
- Bonding powder – Use Super Mend Bonding Powder to attach the fibres to other substances such as fabric. Sprinkle powder on the fabric, lay on the fibres, cover with parchment and iron.

If you want more ideas for using Angelina Fibres, there is a useful book called Between The Sheets With Angelina (see the book list for details).

Shrink plastic

Shrink plastic is another amazing substance that requires heat to work its magic. It comes in sheet form and you can get it in different colours, including white, black, frosted and clear.

To use the shrink plastic, stamp on an image with a StazOn ink pad (see chapter 4). Colour in the stamp with non-alcohol pens, such as the Sakura Gelly Roll range (see chapter 8), and cut around the outline of the image. Hold the image with long tweezers against a heat-proof craft sheet (see chapter 6) and heat with a heat gun. The shape will gradually shrink as it melts. Don't panic as it starts to curl – it will eventually unfold itself if you hold tight! Once the shape has stopped shrinking, flatten it out by pressing it gently with an acrylic block. The end result is a perfect plastic miniature of your stamped image.

Remember that the colours will intensify as the plastic shrinks. A thinly coloured section will become much stronger in miniature – so aim to make your colouring in lighter than usual. You may also want to use a grey or sepia coloured inkpad for stamping, rather than jet-black.

For a useful video tutorial, search for 'Joanna Sheen shrink plastic' on YouTube.

More bits and pieces

Believe it or not, the embellishments we have covered in this chapter are by no means a complete list! As you explore what is available, you will discover many other bits and pieces you can use, such as:

- Tiny coloured pompoms for a clown's hat
- Miniature metal coat hangers for cut-out dresses
- Miniature wooden pegs for pegging on messages or fixing tiny clothes to a washing line
- Skeleton leaves to add to rustic-style cards
- Googly eyes for sticking onto animals, teddy bears or cartoon characters
- Feathers for adding to hats, or for dressing up bird images
- Miniature jingle bells for Christmas cards

Summing Up

- Flat-backed gems and pearls, buttons, bows, ribbons, lace, raffia, string and Baker's Twine are useful for adding that all-important finishing touch to a card.
- For a metallic addition, brads, eyelets and charms work well. Brads can also be used as a decorative way of joining card, paper and sheet material – particularly vellum and acetate.
- A ready-made topper is useful for creating quick and simple cards – and die cut decorated shapes can provide themed embellishments for a wide variety of special occasion cards.
- Decoupage, pyramage and invertage are popular papercrafting techniques that result in beautiful embellishments for a card. You can use ready-printed decoupage sheets, or try decoupaging stamped images and photographs.
- Angelina Fibres is an iridescent polyester substance that fuses when it is heated to create a crisp, shimmering sheet material. An Angelina sheet can be cut, stamped or moulded.
- Shrink plastic is tremendous fun to use and it enables you to make miniature stamped and coloured embellishments for your cards.

Chapter Eight

Some More Effects

So far, we have looked at creating different effects using the key techniques of embossing and stencilling. In this chapter we explore the many other effects that can be used in card making.

Glitter, glitter glue and micro-beads

Glitter, glitter glue and micro-beads are great for adding colour, texture and sparkle to your projects.

'Glitter, glitter glue and micro-beads are great for adding colour, texture and sparkle to your projects.'

Glitter

Glitter is made up of tiny iridescent flecks. It comes in a huge range of colours and most glitters have a metallic sheen. Gold and silver are particularly useful – and you can also get colour mixes, pastel colours, pearlescent glitter, holographic glitter and clear glitter that adds a sugar coating to a coloured surface.

Glitters are not all created equal – and it really is worth buying the very best quality you can afford. There is a huge difference between specialised craft glitter and the cheap tubes of silver, gold, red and green sold in newsagents and toyshops. Like embossing powder (see chapter 6), glitter comes in different grades. Go for fine or micro-fine, unless you particularly want the rough surface effect of a chunkier glitter. Martha Stewart Crafts, Woodware, Stampendous and Art Institute are just some of the companies that make craft glitters. When choosing glitter, search for the colour and finish you want and then, as always, check online reviews to see if it is good quality (Amazon.co.uk or Amazon.com carry reviews for most products).

Using glitter – the basics

The basic process of using glitter is very simple. Place glue on a card or paper background, sprinkle plenty of glitter over the glued area and shake off the excess. The glitter will stick to wherever you have applied the glue to create a sparkly shape or pattern.

A good all-purpose craft glue, such as tacky PVA or Pinflair Glue Gel (www.pinflair.co.uk) is fine for glitter – and if you want to create detail, use a Sakura Quickie Glue pen.

Using glitter – some practical tips

Containing glitter

The number one tip for using glitter is to work on a surface that collects the excess glitter and enables you to return it to the pot. The simplest approach is a piece of copier paper that can be folded into a chute for pouring back the glitter.

Some crafters like to work over a coffee filter paper when glittering small areas. The cup shape catches and contains the loose glitter and can then be poured back into the pot. You can also buy a plastic Tidy Tray, which has curved sides and a built in funnel at one end.

Applying glitter

The most important thing is to make sure that you cover the glue with a generous quantity of glitter – and sprinkle it on before the glue starts to dry. Don't worry if you appear to have drowned the image – the glitter will only stick to the glued sections.

If you are glittering a single shape with one colour on a blank piece of card, you can carefully shake the glitter directly from the pot. There are, however, occasions when you need to control the flow of glitter. For example, if you are adding small finishing touches to an otherwise completed card, you don't want to smother the card with glitter as it will get caught in the other embellishments. For a more controlled flow, try the following:

- Many craft glitters are sold in pots with a movable top that gives you the option of pouring or shaking the glitter. Make sure you move the top round to the part with the holes.
- Buy some cheap salt shakers with large holes for storing your favourite glitters (reusing a shaker for different colours can be tricky as the colours mix).
- Scoop the glitter from the pot with a teaspoon and sprinkle it carefully onto the glued area.

Pressing down the glitter

Gently press down on the glitter with your fingertips to make sure it is packed onto the glue. This is particularly important if you are using a dry adhesive.

Clingy glitter

Glitter can become static and cling to the unglued parts of the paper – a particular problem with fine and micro-fine glitters. The problem of static, clingy glitter can be addressed in the same way as clingy embossing powder – see chapter 6.

Clearing up glitter

Glitter is notorious for getting everywhere! If you like using glitter, you will have to live with it to some extent – but a Scor-Pal product called The Glitter Clean Up Cloth can help considerably. The cloth has an open weave that attracts and traps glitter, embossing powder, mica powder and chalk, making it much easier to wipe your surfaces clean. The cloth is available from www.joannasheen.co.uk, amongst other places.

Using glitter – some techniques

There are many different techniques for applying glitter to your cards:

Double-sided adhesive tape and sheets

Using extra-strong red double-sided tape, place a strip on a piece of background card and remove the protective paper. Sprinkle glitter over the sticky surface, press down gently with the fingertips and shake away the excess. Brush over with a soft make-up brush to get rid of any particles that are still clinging and admire the beautiful sparkly ribbon you have just created. Experiment with different widths of tape to make thick and thin strips.

Punch or cut shapes from a double-sided adhesive sheet to create glittery motifs. You can either stick the shapes onto card before glittering, or leave the protective paper intact on one side to make glittery stickers for future use.

Glittering die cut or punched shapes

Glitter makes an effective decoration for punched or die cut shapes, such as the Grungeboard Elements (see chapter 3). Simply cover the shape with glue and sprinkle on glitter.

For a quick and easy way of glittering lots of shapes, you can also use the glitter bag or glitter box technique. Put the glitter in a freezer bag and pop in the glue-covered shapes, making sure they are well buried in glitter. Alternatively, put an entire pot of glitter in a plastic box, hold the shapes with tweezers and dab them into the glitter. Use these techniques to make a batch of shapes, some for now and some to save for future cards.

Glitter stamping

For this technique, you will need a glue pad. This is similar to an ink pad – except that it comes with a refill bottle and you apply fresh glue whenever you want to use the pad. The Tsukineko Essential Glue Pad is readily available, and their website includes a useful advice section on how to use the glue pad with glitter (click on 'Tips and Techniques' at www.tsukineko.com).

To make glittered stamps, follow these steps:

1. Work on paper or card that is not too absorbent, such as vellum or a coated cardstock.
2. Apply a good quantity of glue to the pad.
3. Press your rubber or clear stamp on the glue pad.
4. Stamp the glued image onto the card or paper background.
5. Sprinkle with fine glitter.
6. Carefully press on the glitter with a clear acrylic block (see chapter 4), to make sure it is well stuck down.
7. Shake off the excess glitter and leave to dry for at least 10 minutes.
8. Clean the glue off your stamps straightaway, using a stamp cleaner (see chapter 4).

You can either leave the glittered stamped image as an outline or fill in the sections with glue and add more glitter. You can also carefully colour in the sections with Sakura Gelly Roll pens (see chapter 8).

'If you heat emboss a stamped image, the raised lines make it easier to keep the glittered sections separate from each other.'

Colouring in stamped images with glitter

Using a Sakura Quickie Glue pen, apply glue to the inner sections of a stamped image and sprinkle with glitter. Make sure you glue and glitter each section, before moving on to the next. It can be hard to prevent one section of glitter from bleeding into another, particularly when you are new to the technique; get round this obstacle by choosing colours that blend well together (blues, purples and pinks or reds, oranges and yellows). This technique also works well for images that suit blended colours, such as butterflies, dragonflies and flowers.

If you heat emboss a stamped image, the raised lines make it easier to keep the glittered sections separate from each other. Glitter glue is also useful for colouring in stamped images – see chapter 4.

Colouring in outline peel-offs with glitter

Glitter makes an effective medium for colouring in the sections of an outline peel-off stamp. For more on this technique, see chapter 5.

Glittering double-sided adhesive peel-offs

This technique produces a similar effect to glitter stamping. Stick the peel-off on the card background, remove the protective paper and apply glitter in the same way as with double-sided tape (see previous section on page 132).

Glittered details

Tiny glittered details can be created using a Sakura Quickie Glue pen. Make dots, lines, shapes and words with the glue pen and sprinkle over with glitter. This is a useful technique if you want to highlight tiny details – such as the lines on a butterfly's wing, or dots on patterned paper.

Glittering on acetate

You will need either an outline peel-off sticker (see chapter 5) or a rubber stamp and black StazOn ink pad (see chapter 4). A black outline sticker looks good for designs using more than one colour glitter. Either buy a sheet of black stickers or colour a gold or silver sticker with a black ProMarker (see page 140).

If you want to use just a single glitter colour, gold and silver outlines look pretty. Try gold with a warm coloured glitter such as red, yellow or orange, and silver with a cold coloured glitter such as turquoise, sea-green or violet. Gold outlines with gold glitter and silver outlines with silver glitter can also look surprisingly effective.

To glitter an image on acetate, follow these steps and pointers:

- Stamp or stick your image to the acetate.
- Turn the acetate over as you will be working on the back of the image.
- Apply tacky PVA glue to a section of the image. You can squeeze the glue directly from the nozzle, or use a pokey tool or glue pen to manoeuvre the glue into tight, intricate areas.
- Don't worry if the glue creeps onto the lines of the image – it won't show as you are working from behind. Do, however, make sure that the glue doesn't stray from one section to another, or you will end up with patches of glitter in the wrong places.

- Apply glitter as usual and move on to the next section.
- If you are using the same coloured glitter in different sections of the image, glue and glitter them in one go.
- When you have finished, leave the project until bone dry and then turn it over to admire the stunning glazed, glittery effect you have created.

Cut around the outline of the glittered shape and stick it to a background. You can also cut out the shape within an acetate square or rectangle. Stick the acetate square to a cut-out frame, and mount the frame on the card front with foam tape. This raises the acetate from the surface of your card, helping to bring out the sparkle of the glittered image.

Glittering with lace

This is one of those techniques that is simple to do, but gives fabulous results. You will need a wide piece of lace (flat synthetic lace works best), a sheet of double-sided adhesive paper or a large sticky label and two contrasting shades of glitter (such as pale pearlescent pink and deep red). To make the glittered lace pattern, follow these steps:

1. Peel off the backing paper to reveal the sticky surface of the label or double-sided adhesive sheet.
2. Stick the lace onto the sheet, smooth side facing downwards.
3. Sprinkle the pink glitter all over the lace-covered sticky sheet and gently rub it in. Make sure that the glitter is worked into all the open parts of the lace design.
4. Shake off the excess glitter and peel away the lace to reveal the pink glittery pattern. The lace acts as a resist, protecting the covered parts of the pattern so that they remain unglittered and sticky.
5. Sprinkle on the red glitter, and work it gently into the sheet with your fingertips before shaking off the excess. The red glitter will stick to the remaining sticky sections, filling in the pattern created by the pink glitter to create a sparkly two-tone effect.

If you want to watch how this is done, there is a useful video tutorial on YouTube called 'Glitter Lace Resist Technique'.

Glitter glue

Glitter glue, as its name suggests, is a clear glue mixed with particles of glitter. It can be used for colouring in stamped or peel-off images and creating lines, dots and blobs of glitter on a background of card or sturdy paper. Glitter glue usually comes in a squeezable bottle with a nozzle. Tim Holtz Stickles Glitter Glue has a fine-tipped nozzle, enabling you to control the flow of glue. The Stickles range includes Ice Stickles, with chunkier particles of glitter, and Distress Stickles which creates a variegated, matte effect in-keeping with the distressed style of crafting.

Micro-beads

'Micro-beads (sometimes referred to as accent beads) are tiny coloured spheres that can be used in a similar way to glitter.'

Micro-beads (sometimes referred to as accent beads) are tiny coloured spheres that can be used in a similar way to glitter. To decorate punched or die cut shapes with micro-beads, cover the shape with a good layer of tacky glue, sprinkle on the beads and then shake off the excess. You can also sprinkle the beads onto double-sided tape (preferably the super strong red kind). If the beads don't completely cover the adhesive, sprinkle on some glitter to fill in the gaps.

Another easy and effective technique is to sprinkle micro beads onto UTEE while it is still hot (see chapter 6) or Glossy Accents (see page 144) before it has dried.

Bouncing beads!

Micro-beads are very bouncy and have a tendency to escape. Work on a tray with raised sides or even a large flat plastic box.

Flower Soft and flocking powder

Flower Soft is a good name for this substance as it is very soft and looks like flower blossoms. Flower Soft is made up of tiny coloured fragments. It is used just like glitter; apply glue to your card, sprinkle on the Flower Soft and shake off the excess. It's important to use a good layer of tacky PVA glue or, better still, Flower Soft's own version which is contained in a small bottle with a fine-tipped applicator.

Flower Soft comes tightly packed into small, clear plastic containers. Once it has been opened, the Flower Soft expands, making it hard to get back into the original container. Many card makers decant Flower Soft into a lidded plastic box and use the original pots for something else (crafters never throw anything away!) A little goes a long way; you may want to consider sharing pots with a crafting friend so you can buy twice as many colours for the same price.

Flower Soft provides a unique texture to add to your cards. It comes in a range of colours, including single and mixed colours, and it's great for creating effects such as textured yellow daisy centres, green foliage for trees (use a mix of different shades for a natural effect), white fluffy snow, a sheep's woolly coat, cupcake frosting and animal fur. For more information and to buy Flower Soft products, go to www.flower-soft.co.uk.

'Liquid Appliqué competes with heat embossing as one of the most satisfying of all the card making techniques.'

Flocking powder

Flocking powder (sometimes called flock) is made up of tiny coloured fibres. It is used in much the same way as Flower Soft, except that it creates a smoother, more velvety texture. It can be sprinkled and pressed onto an image stamped with a glue pad, or used in the same way as glitter on double-sided adhesive tape or transparent peel-offs.

You can also use flocking powder to create a velvety surface for matting and layering (see chapter 10). Cover a piece of card with tacky PVA glue, sprinkle on the flock and press down with the fingertips. For a sparkly effect, mix glitter with the flocking powder.

Liquid Appliqué

Marvy Uchida Liquid Appliqué is a thick, gloopy substance that comes in a tube with a nozzle at the end. When you first squeeze the Liquid Appliqué out of the tube, it looks rather dull. This, however, is only the start of the process. Once you have applied it to your project, heat it with a heat gun – and watch in amazement as it slowly puffs up to create a fluffy marshmallow texture. Liquid Appliqué competes with heat embossing as one of the most satisfying of all the card-making techniques.

Liquid Appliqué can be used in similar ways to Flower Soft – although it makes an even more convincing snow or cupcake frosting! It also works well for creating textured scarves, mittens, woolly hats and the furry white cuffs on Father Christmas's robe. It comes in various colours – and you can also sprinkle on glitter before heating to create a sparkly raised motif.

Alcohol inks

'Alcohol inks can be used to make colourful, free-form backgrounds – and they are great fun to explore and mess about with.'

Alcohol inks come in bottles rather than ink pads. They are a transparent, vibrant and fast-drying ink that can be used to create a number of different effects. Alcohol inks work best on non-porous surfaces such as glossy card, acetate, vellum or metal.

Using alcohol inks

Alcohol inks can be used to make colourful, free-form backgrounds – and they are great fun to explore and mess about with. The following suggestions will get you started:

Using inks with an ink blending tool

Squeeze spots of ink from the bottles into the felt pad of the blending tool and dab onto glossy card. The coloured inks will blend on the glossy surface of the card to create a beautiful smudgy pattern.

Using the mixatives

Shake the bottle vigorously to make sure the contents are well mixed before applying tiny dots to the felt pad (along with the alcohol inks). Dab onto the glossy card to make a smudgy pattern with flashes of metallic or pearlescent colour.

Using the blending solution

Apply the blending solution to the blending tool felt pad and dab on inked card. The solution lightens and further blends the coloured inks – and if you have included a mixative, it brings out the metallic or pearlescent effects. You can also drip blending solution onto the inked card to create bleached areas.

Building up colour intensity

Dab ink over the card and leave to dry before reapplying the ink to the blending tool and dabbing for a second time. If you want to make the colours even more intense, repeat the process a third time.

Creating feathery patterns

Drip alcohol inks, a little mixative and blending solution onto a non-stick crafting sheet to make a puddle. Rub the glossy surface of the card over the inks to create a feathery pattern.

Creating watery patterns

Using a water spray bottle, spritz a glossy card to make the surface wet. Dab on inks with the blender tool to create a light, watery effect.

Stamping on an alcohol ink background

Alcohol ink backgrounds make a beautiful foil for stamped images. A simple, bold stamp used with a Ranger's Archival ink pad works well. You can also heat emboss on an alcohol ink background. Using a Versamark ink pad, stamp and emboss your image. Choose embossing powder in a colour that will show up against the inked background – or create a more subtle effect with a powder that is similar in colour to the inks.

Using alcohol inks on other surfaces

Alcohol ink used on vellum and acetate creates a beautiful translucent effect. You can also experiment with other surfaces, such as rubbing your inked blending tool across crumpled tin foil.

Try this – inking the edge of the card

The ink blending tool is useful for inking round the edges of a card – although you get a softer look if you dab the blending tool onto an ink pad, rather than using it with alcohol inks. Inking round the edge of a card gives an attractive, shadowy effect. It also adds definition and hides a slightly wobbly cut. To ink the edges of a card, follow these steps:

- Set out your materials and equipment on a non-stick craft sheet.
- Dab your ink blending tool onto the ink pad and then dab it on the craft sheet to remove some of the ink.
- Using a gentle circular motion and working inwards, dust the ink around the edges of your card.

Make sure you use the straight edge of the felt pad, rather than the corner. Some crafters prefer to remove the felt pad from the blending tool and use it by itself.

You can also use chalk and small chalk ink pads such as Versamagic or ColorBox for this technique. To create yet another look, try inking or chalking along a torn edge.

'Colouring pens are an invaluable card-making resource. They are particularly useful for colouring in stamped images and outline stickers.'

Colouring pens

Colouring pens are an invaluable card-making resource. They are particularly useful for colouring in stamped images and outline stickers.

As always, it is important to use high-quality pens to get a good result. The following brands are among the most popular and reliable:

ProMarkers

ProMarkers are permanent pens that can be used on glossy surfaces, as well as paper and card. Because they are alcohol-based, they tend to smudge if you use them with other solvent-based inks, such as StazOn (see chapter 4). If you want to use ProMarkers for colouring in a stamped image, go for a water-based ink pad. Letraset, who make ProMarkers, recommend the Tsukineko Memento ink pad.

The ink in a ProMarker is transparent, and can be built up in layers to create shading. Once you have coloured in a section of your image, go over parts of it again to get a darker shade. ProMarkers produce a fine layer of colour with no streaks – they really do look as though they have been printed, as long as you work on a good-quality, smooth paper. They come with a fine bullet nib at one end for precision work and a wide chisel tip at the other end for larger areas.

You can also buy a ProMarker blending pen. Use it to soften the edges of your colouring, blend colours together and create pale patterns within an area of colour. For a useful illustrated introduction to using ProMarkers, visit www.promarker.info.

Copic Markers

There are two types of Copic Marker:

- The standard marker with a fine nib at one end and a chisel nib at the other.
- The Copic Sketch Marker, with a broad nib at one end and a brush tip for smooth strokes at the other.

Like ProMarkers, Copic Markers are alcohol-based and can be used on a wide range of surfaces – including glossy card and acetate. They are refillable and the nibs are replaceable.

Sakura Gelly Roll pens

These are the original gel pen, and they come in a wide range of effects, including:

- Gelly Roll Gel Pens – the basic gel pen, in fine-point or medium-point
- Gelly Roll Metallic – a range of colours with a pearly, metallic sheen
- Gelly Roll Stardust – glittery

- Gelly Roll Shadow – two-tone, with a gold or silver line alongside the colour
- Gelly Roll Moonlight – fluorescent
- Soufflé and Glaze – these unique pens create raised lines and can be used on non-porous surfaces such as vellum and acetate, as well as paper and card. The Soufflé is opaque and shows up well on dark surfaces. The Glaze is translucent and looks particularly effective on acetate

For a visual demonstration of all the Sakura pens and what you can do with them, there is a useful YouTube tutorial called 'Sakura Fanatic with Joanne Fink'.

Chalks

'Crafting chalk is a beautiful medium that can be used to add a soft, misty colour to your projects.'

Crafting chalk is a beautiful medium that can be used to add a soft, misty colour to your projects. Crafting chalks come in small pans, a bit like solid water colours paints. The chalk is applied to the surface of the paper with a sponge applicator. You can also use a cotton bud, or for larger areas, a cotton wool ball, a sponge or even a clean finger.

Tips for using chalks

- Work on paper with a matte surface.
- Use a gentle, circular motion to apply the colour.
- Use the chalk sparingly – you can always add more.
- Create a richer colour by adding layers.
- A good-quality artist's eraser can be used to remove small quantities of chalk from your project.
- Experiment with blending chalks to get new colours, or blending one area of colour into the edge of another.
- Practise with blending on rough paper, before using the chalks on your actual project.
- Chalk does not stick to the paper, so it needs to be fixed with a special spray fixative, or hairspray from an aerosol can.

- Some chalks are described as non-smudge – which means they shouldn't need fixing. However, it's a good idea to double check, particularly with a card you want to sell or send in the post.
- Chalks can also be used with a wet paint brush. This will give you a stronger colour and a less smudgy effect.

Mica powders, paints and sprays

Mica powders, paints and sprays have tiny flakes of mica added to give a unique, sparkly sheen.

Mica powders and paints

The three brands you are most likely to come across are:

- Ranger's Perfect Pearls
- Cosmic Shimmer Powder
- Luminarte's Twinkling H20s

Perfect Pearls and Cosmic Shimmer are small pots of intensely coloured pigment powder, whereas the Twinkling H20s come as a dry cake of paint. To use the powders, tip a tiny amount onto a white waterproof surface (many crafters use a white plate or ceramic tile) and mix with a small amount of water. To use the Twinkling H20s, spritz the cake with water and leave to soften before lifting off the colour with a brush. If you buy a set of H20s, they should come with a spritzer bottle.

Once the mica pigment has been mixed with water, it can be painted onto stamped images or the inside sections of outline peel-off. Mica powders are at their most effective on darker backgrounds. For techniques using mica powders with stamps, see chapter 4.

Mica sprays

Mica sprays create a beautiful speckled look. The mica in the spray produces a similar shimmer to the mica powders, but the effect is more light and misty. Like mica powders, mica sprays work best on dark or black card, as this makes the colours glow. Use the sprays on the thickest card possible; they are quite wet and can cause lightweight card and paper to wrinkle.

Two of the most popular mica sprays are Cosmic Shimmer Mist and Perfect Pearls Mists (spray versions of the powders). Both come in a wide range of colours, and both need to be shaken extensively to make sure that the pigment and the mica flakes are distributed throughout the liquid.

Mica sprays can be misted across a stencil or sprayed randomly over card to make a glimmering background. Try spraying different colours across crumpled tissue paper for a visually interesting distressed effect.

'Mica sprays can be misted across a stencil or sprayed randomly over card to make a glimmering background.'

Glossy Accents and other clear glazes

Clear glaze is useful for adding a glossy finish to a surface.

Glossy Accents

Inkssentials Glossy Accents is a very thick, clear glaze that dries to a hard, glassy finish. It comes in a bottle with a fine tip, enabling you to glaze tiny details on an image, or create dewdrop effects. If you want to cover a larger area, you can use the nozzle to spread it out over your surface. Don't worry if it looks a bit ruffled; it has a thick, viscous texture and will gradually find its own level. Keep a pin handy as the liquid dries in the nozzle, and you need to clean it out before each use.

You can add glitter to wet Glossy Accents or add colour by mixing in alcohol inks. You do, however, need to handle it with care. Once air bubbles are trapped inside the liquid, it's very difficult to get rid of them. Avoid shaking the bottle, and if you mix in inks or glitters, make sure you don't also stir in air. If you do get an air bubble when you apply the Glossy Accents, try dragging it out of the wet glaze with a cocktail stick or pokey tool. Because Glossy Accents is so viscous, it can take a long time to dry. Projects with a thick coating are best left to dry overnight.

Glossy Accents can be applied to any surface. Use it on patterned paper, alcohol ink backgrounds, card sprayed with shimmer mists, stamped and coloured images and punched and die cut shapes. You can also use Glossy Accents to glaze a paper or fabric blossom. To add some sparkle to the blossom, try sprinkling glitter or micro-beads over the tips of the petals while they are still wet.

Try this – making faux jewels

Make faux gems and pearls by putting blobs of Glossy Accents on circles punched from glitter or pearlescent card.

Crackle Accents

Crackle Accents is similar to Glossy Accents, except that it creates a crackled effect as it dries. It is a useful medium for adding a weathered look to your cards.

Decoupage glaze

Projects such as decoupage (see chapter 7) require a glazed sheen, but without the dimension of Glossy Accents. There are many thinner glazes to choose from. Pinflair Craft Glaze is good for brushing over a wide range of surfaces, and the integral brush makes it easy to apply to your project. If you want to glaze decoupage images, brush over them and leave to dry for about 20 minutes before cutting or popping them out their sheet. There is a useful YouTube demo on glazing decoupage images, called 'How do I use Pinflair Craft Glaze?'

Summing Up

- Glitter and glitter glue can be used in many different ways to add sparkle to a card. The technique for using Flower Soft and flocking powder is similar to that of glitter, although their soft textures create a completely different effect. Puffy Liquid Appliqué offers yet another texture to explore.
- Alcohol inks can be used with a blending tool and blending solution to create some fabulous, colourful background effects on glossy card, acetate and vellum.
- Alcohol pens such as ProMarkers and gel pens such as the Sakura Gelly Roll range are must-have crafting items, particularly if you want to colour in stamped images or outline peel-offs.
- Mica powders and sprays create beautiful, shimmering effects. The powders can be used for stamping projects and mixed with UTEE, and the sprays make stunning backgrounds, particularly when used on dark card.
- Glossy Accents and other craft glazes can be used to add a clear, glassy sheen to background papers, embellishments and decoupage.

Chapter Nine

Words and Sentiments

If you are making a card for a specific event, such as a birthday, an anniversary or a new baby, you may want to add a sentiment. There are many different ways of incorporating words into the design of your card – and many ways of representing those words.

Ways of producing words

Unless you have unusually good handwriting, or you want to practise your calligraphy skills, you will need to choose a technique for adding words to your cards.

'Peel-off stickers offer a quick and easy way of adding a sentiment.'

Peel-offs

Peel-off stickers offer a quick and easy way of adding a sentiment. There is a huge choice available, with everything from the standard 'Happy Birthday' to more unusual messages such as 'Across The Miles'. Craft Creations (www.craftcreations.co.uk) have a good selection, and the Anita's brand of peel-offs is also worth looking out for. You can either get sheets of identical sentiments or sheets with a variety of sentiments on a theme – for example, a collection of messages suitable for Christmas cards.

Peel-off sentiments are quick to use – although they can look as though they have been stuck on as an afterthought. Always plan how to fit a sentiment into the design of your card. Matting and layering the peel-off, colouring it with alcohol pens or even using it as a stencil will help it to blend into your overall design.

Sentiment peel-offs can be tricky to manoeuvre, particularly if they are long. Once you have decided where to place the peel-off, it's important to get it level. Stick a yellow post-it note on your card and use it as a line guide for positioning the sentiment.

You can also get single letters – sometimes called alphabet peel-offs. These are more fiddly to use than word peel-offs as you have to position each letter separately. They do, however, enable you to write whatever you want, and they are also much more versatile. See page 150 for some ideas on how to use single letters.

Alphabet peel-offs come in various different font styles and sizes. Craft Creations do tiny print-style letters in both lower and upper case - which is handy if you want to fit a message into a small space on your card. As an alternative, Anita's do large, ornate letters which can be used as the focal point of a card.

Stamps

If you can't find the right words as a peel-off, the chances are there is a sentiment stamp that will fit the bill! The stamp designer is able to use whatever font style they wish, and also arrange the words artistically; for example, a circular sentiment design can look very effective, as can words combined with little motifs.

Unlike peel-offs, a stamp design can also include as many words as required. Some messages are cute, some are humorous, some are quirky and some are heart-warming. The right stamped message can make a good focal point for your card, particularly if you use techniques such as glittering, heat embossing or chalk resist.

Try this – rainbow words

Using either your computer or a sentiment stamp, print a single word or phrase several times to form a column. Use different coloured ink for each print to create a rainbow effect. This works well for short words or phrases, such as 'birthday' or 'thank you'.

Perhaps the one disadvantage of sentiment stamps is the need for a huge collection to cover all occasions. As with peel-offs, alphabet stamps provide an alternative in enabling you to come up with the exact words you want. Single letter stamps are available in a variety of styles, ranging from unusual fonts such as old fashioned typewriter keys and scrabble tiles to ornate calligraphy and simple print-style letters.

'The right stamped message can make a good focal point for your card.'

Using single letter stamps and peel-offs – some tips

The following ideas are just a few ways of using alphabet stamps and peel-offs:

- If you use unmounted stamps and a large acrylic block, you can place the whole word on the block, rather than stamping each letter separately. Remember to position the letters backwards, or you will end up with a word in mirror writing. Always do a try-out on rough paper to make sure the letters are where they should be – and that everything is spelt correctly!
- When you want to stamp a word on a cut-out circle, square or rectangle, mark the middle letter in your word (such as 'p' in 'happy') and stamp it in the centre of the shape. You can then stamp the remaining letters on either side to fill the space. If you want the letters to be level, use a post-it note as a line guide – although letters with a slight zigzag can look effective, particularly within a circle. The same technique is also useful for positioning peel-off letters to make a word.

- An even easier (and effective) way of positioning single letters is to stamp or stick them onto small punched circles, squares, hearts or stars before sticking them onto your card. If you have alphabet sets in different fonts, try mixing and matching them to create words with a quirky look.
- If you have alphabet stamps that print large, simple letters, you can cut them out to create your own stickers. Although this is more time-consuming than stamping onto card or paper shapes, it gives you another way of using your letter stamps.
- Any of the techniques described in chapters 4 and 5 can be used to decorate the stamped or peel-off words on your card.

Try this – letter bunting

Cut out isosceles triangles of paper in patterns and colours that work well together. Choose a word such as 'birthday' or 'celebrate', and print or stick peel-off letters onto each flag to spell the word. If necessary, colour gold or silver peel-offs with a black peel-off marker, to make sure they show up. Stick them across a card to make bunting.

Glue pens, glitter and heat embossing

As long as your handwriting is good enough, writing a message with a Sakura Quickie Glue pen and glittering the letters can look very effective. You can also heat emboss a message if you write it with a glue or embossing pen (see chapter 6).

Die cut sentiments

Die cut sentiments are card shapes with printed messages. The shapes are usually sold in sheets, and to use them you simply pop a sentiment out of the sheet and stick it onto your card.

Die cut sentiments come in a huge range of styles and shapes, and they are quick and easy to use. On the downside, it's hard to make a die cut sentiment look unique, as all you have to do is decide where on the card front to put it. Because they can only be used once, good-quality sentiments also work out quite expensive.

Printing your own sentiments

Printing out your own sentiments is great fun, as long as you have a good printer. This technique enables you to choose exactly the letter size, word arrangement, font style and colour that is right for your card design. You can also print onto any substance that your printer will accept, including vellum and printable acetate.

Bear in mind that words can appear very different on screen. Print out a small sample to check how the size, colour and font look on paper – and then print the complete sentiment in draft, to make sure it fits into your design. If you are not sure about size, print out a few different sized words in draft – but make sure you type the font size number alongside each word, so you can identify the one you want to use.

'Die cut sentiments come in a huge range of styles and shapes, and they are quick and easy to use.'

Sentiments on craft CDs

Some craft CDs include sentiments and messages that you can print out. This is a useful facility, as the content and design of the sentiments will match the design and theme of the images, toppers and background papers on the CD. For more on craft CDs, see chapter 3.

Grungeboard, chipboard and other die cut letters

You can buy ready-cut individual letters in a variety of materials, including Grungeboard, chipboard, card, foam and plastic. Grungeboard and chipboard letters can be inked, embossed, glittered, sanded or covered in paper (for more on decorating Grungeboard and chipboard, see chapter 3).

Die cut letters are quite expensive, and they can only be used once. As they tend to come in an alphabet set, you can also find yourself running out of some letters while others never get used. A cheaper option is to use the letters as a template. Draw round them on paper or card and cut out the letters with scissors or a craft knife. If you want the special qualities of Grungeboard, use your templates on a plain sheet of Grungeboard or Grungepaper.

Using letters, words and sentiments on your cards

There are endless ways of building letters, words and sentiments into your card designs. The following are just a few suggestions to get you started:

Large initials

'A large single word works well as the main embellishment for a card.'

A large initial is a lovely way of personalising a card. Use a die cut letter and make it the central feature of your card, decorating it in a style that will appeal to the recipient. As an alternative to using a die cut letter, download a letter template from the Internet. If you want some ideas on how to decorate the letter, do an Internet image search for 'handmade initial cards'.

Large single words

A large single word works well as the main embellishment for a card. Choose one or two words, such as 'Eid Mubarak' (the Muslim greeting during the Eid festivals) and cut out large letters from patterned paper. You can mix and match patterns or choose a single pattern for the letters. Create a matted and layered background with borders along the top and bottom of the card, carefully position the letters on the card (making sure they are evenly spaced) and stick them down to complete the card.

3D letters

Stick large, die cut letters onto the card front with foam pads, to give a three-dimensional look. Colour and pattern the letters to match the theme of the card; glitter them for Christmas, cover with pale blue or pink paper and add white spots for a new baby card, cover with striped paper in masculine colours for a man's birthday card.

Matting and layering sentiments

The most straightforward way of making a sentiment look special is to mat and layer it (see chapter 10). Cut out your sentiment and mount it on two or three layers of contrasting card, paper, ribbon or other sheet material. The sentiment can then be added wherever it looks best – along the top or the bottom, to the side, in the centre, at an angle . . . Experiment with different places on the card, to make sure it is just where you want it before sticking it down.

You can also be creative with your matting and layering. Try the following ideas:

- Mount your sentiment on a torn strip of vellum.
- Cut out words within a strip of card, and mount the strip across a card circle or oval in a contrasting colour.
- Attach a mounted sentiment to the card front using decorative brads at each end.
- Punch or die cut a series of nesting shapes, add your sentiment to the smallest shape and layer the larger shapes to make a background.
- Mount the final word in a phrase – for example, 'You are a Star', with the word 'Star' mounted or printed onto a star shape.

Speech bubbles

Mounting your sentiment onto a speech bubble or a thought bubble is a fun way of adding words to your card. This technique works well for cards with cute cartoon characters, or animal cards aimed at children.

Try this – Thinking of You

Using a cute character stamp (such as a teddy bear), stamp, colour and cut out the image. Stick the character to the centre of your card and add a 'Thinking of You' or 'Missing You' thought bubble. Add other small embellishments such as stamped or punched flowers, small hearts or glittered stars.

Tickertape

Using tickertape to add wording can look very effective. The easiest technique is to print out a repeated word on card or paper and cut it into a strip to stick along the bottom, or top and bottom of your card. This technique works best with just one or two words, rather than a whole message. Don't worry about cutting a word in half at the edge of the card – this makes the tickertape look more realistic.

'Mounting your sentiment onto a speech bubble or a thought bubble is a fun way of adding words to your card.'

Tags and labels

Mounting a sentiment on a tag or luggage label is an easy and effective way of adding words to your card. Punch a hole in the tip of the tag and thread with ribbon or twine. Turn the tag into a feature by adding other little embellishments, such as a brad, a charm or a bow. The tag can also be designed to fit in with the overall look of your card; for example, stamped, sprayed and sanded for a distressed style card, pale pink with lace trim for a baby girl card or plain brown cardboard to go with natural embellishments such as handmade paper, hessian and buttons.

Use an actual luggage label as a template for your tag. Alternatively, you can buy different sized and coloured tags from www.craftcreations.com, use a tag-shaped paper punch or invest in tag-shaped dies for a die cutting machine. Some crafting CDs include tags that you can print and cut out.

Try this – a personalised Christmas card

A tag is a good way of breaking up a vertical design with a horizontal element. Create a personalised Christmas card by sticking gold ribbon down the centre of a DL card. Make a tag to stick to the centre of the ribbon so that it overlaps the edge of the card. Print out your own message for the tag and thread a narrow red or green ribbon through the hole. Punch out holly leaves from lightweight green card and different sized hearts from red glitter paper. Stick the leaves and hearts on top of the ribbon, in a symmetrical arrangement above and below the tag. Mark in the veins of the holly leaves with gold pen and stick tiny sequins stars down the sides of the card.

Down and around the edge

A word doesn't have to be horizontal. Positioning separate letters vertically down the edge of the card can look very effective. This works particularly well with peel-off or printed letters on circles.

Separating single peel-off letters with motifs to make a border around the edge of the card can also look very pretty.

Curved words

Make the most of single peel-off letters to create shaped and curved words. For example, the word 'Birthday' can look very effective hugging the curved side of a flower vase.

'Positioning words around an aperture looks stylish, and also makes the aperture frame look less stark.'

Words round an aperture

Positioning words around an aperture looks stylish, and also makes the aperture frame look less stark. For a square aperture, print out the words on good-quality card or paper, cut into strips and stick one strip along each side. Print draft try-outs to make sure you have the right font and size to fit comfortably around the aperture – and if necessary, repeat shorter words such as 'baby boy' to fill up each side.

For a round or oval aperture, stamp or stick single letters onto shapes and stick around the edge of the aperture.

Word backgrounds

Make a background by repeat typing a word, using a small, simple font and a subtle colour. For example, 'Good Luck' in green covering an entire sheet of card makes an attractive themed background for motifs such as four-leaf clovers, horseshoes and black cats.

Letter backgrounds

Randomly stamping letters on paper or card is another technique for making a background. Backgrounds need to be subtle, and a tone on tone stamping technique helps to soften the stamped letters so that they don't detract from the main embellishment. You can personalise the card by using the initials of the recipient - or use an initial that matches your theme, such as C for Christmas, B for birthday, or X for Valentine cards.

> **Tone on tone**
>
> Tone on tone means using the same coloured ink and paper, but having the ink a little darker so that it shows up without being too dominant.

Printing on acetate

Print out your sentiment on printable acetate, using a strong, dark colour such as black or brown. Choose a subtle patterned paper to go underneath the acetate, cut out the sentiment and attach to the card with brads so that the background pattern shows through.

Different fonts and sizes

Use more than one font within a single phrase. For example, you could print or stamp 'Happy' in an ornate font, followed by a plain font for 'Birthday'. It's also worth thinking about the size of your font. Sometimes, a very small message in a plain font can look effective – and you can also include more than one sentiment using different fonts and sizes within the one card. How about a large, plain 'Happy Birthday' positioned centrally, with a tiny ornate 'It's Your Special Day' in the corner? Play around with different combinations of font size and style – the best card-making effects are often stumbled upon accidentally!

Record a message

For a special card, consider investing in a Darice Record-It Button. This is a small device that can record a ten-second spoken message and play it back with the push of a button. Its flat design means that it can be fixed to a card without creating too much bulk.

Wording for inserts

Although they are not on show, the words inside a card are also important.

Insert greetings

If you order ready-cut inserts from pdacardandcraft.co.uk, you can ask for them to be printed with a greeting. There is a good range to choose from and you can pick from one of four fonts.

You can also print your own messages for inserts, and decorate them to make the inside as beautiful as the outside. Stamped or computer printed messages work well. Some crafting CDs also have printable wording for inserts.

Verses for inserts

If you want to put a verse inside your card, there are a few options:

- Try making up your own verses.
- Borrow a verse from a manufactured card.
- Download a free verse from the Internet – www.craftyco.com has a good choice of verses for lots of different occasions, although not for cards you want to sell.
- Invest in Judith Wibberley's *Just the Right Words: Over 400 Messages and Motifs for Cardmakers and Crafters* (see the book list for details).

It is, however, important that you don't sell cards with borrowed or downloaded verses, or you may end up infringing copyright. For more on copyright and selling your cards, see the next chapter.

Summing Up

- There are lots of different techniques for adding sentiments to your cards, including stamps, peel-offs, ready printed die cut sentiments and die cut letters.
- Typing and printing out words and sentiments enables you to choose your own colour, size, font style and wording.
- Words and sentiments can be central to the card, or a more subtle part of the overall design. Whatever role the sentiment plays in your card, it's important to think through how it fits into the overall design.
- Matting and layering a sentiment, using tags, mounting single letters on shapes, repeating words on tickertape and using printed letters to make backgrounds are just some of the ways you can add words to a card.
- The words inside the card are also important and you can add verses as well as a greeting. Do, however, make sure you don't use verses with a copyright if you plan to sell the cards.

Chapter Ten

Designing and Selling Your Cards

Throughout this book, we've explored the many different techniques and equipment you can use in your card making. In this chapter, we look at how to go about designing a card and where to get ideas and inspiration. We also look at the practicalities of selling your cards if you want to turn your hobby into a small business.

Designing your cards – matting and layering

Matting and layering is a term you will come across regularly in the card-making world. The technique is fundamental to card making – and it gives you a chance to use your beautiful paper, card and sheet materials, as well as effects such as embossing and glittering.

Matting and layering simply means building up different sized backgrounds (mats) in layers, one on top of the other. Matting and layering adds colour, pattern, texture and dimension to your card. It also creates a background and a frame for your main topper or embellishment, helping to draw in the eye.

Matting and layering is one of the most popular and versatile techniques in card making. The simplest form of matting and layering is to stick two or three rectangles or squares on top of each other, working from largest to smallest.

Once you've mastered the basics of matting and layering, the sky's the limit as to how many different designs you can come up with. Your mats can be any shape or size, and they don't have to sit one on top of the other. You can set them at an angle, arrange them around the card front, overlap different shapes and combine large shapes with narrow bands of card or paper.

'Matting and layering adds colour, pattern, texture and dimension to your card.'

Perfect matting and layering

To get perfectly measured margins between your mats, use a clear gridded metal edged ruler and a craft knife. This enables you to line up and cut each mat so that every margin is exactly the same along each edge. For a clear demonstration using the Pinflair metal edge ruler, search on YouTube for 'How do I get perfect matting and layering with Antony's ruler technique?'

Designing your cards – colours, patterns and textures

The key to successful matting and layering lies in your choice of colour, pattern and texture – and how they combine to provide a foil for the main focal point of your card.

'Choosing different textures adds interest to the card and prevents it from looking flat.'

Take your topper or embellishment as a starting point and look at what colours, patterns and textures might suit it. For example:

- If you want to build your card around a flower motif in pale blue and white, go for complementary colours, such as a pale blue patterned paper, white or blue organza ribbon, white hammer card and silver mirri card.
- If the same flower motif is in red and cream, you may decide on a more homespun look – torn-edged handmade paper, a piece of hessian, smooth cream card and red gingham ribbon.

In both of the above examples, the colour scheme is quite limited – blue, white and silver for the first and red, cream and neutrals for the second. It's not, however, just the colour that matters. Choosing different textures adds interest to the card and prevents it from looking flat. In the blue and white example, shiny mirri card contrasts with filmy organza ribbon and stippled hammer card; in the red and cream example, the rough torn edge of the handmade paper and the hairy hessian contrast with the smooth surface of the cream card.

Although they include different colours and a range of textures, both these examples have only the one pattern (blue patterned paper and red gingham ribbon). Introducing just a single pattern into your card design can be easier to start off with, but don't be afraid to play around with mixing patterns. Spots and stripes can look great together as long as the colours work. Florals also go well with spots or stripes, and in some cases with each other. The only rule is whether or not it works for the card designer – you!

Edging your mats

Adding a shaped edge to one or more of your mats is an effective way of introducing texture and pattern to your card design. Use fancy scissors, a paper trimmer with a shaped blade, a die cutting machine or a border punch to create shapes with patterned edges.

Tearing mats is another way of adding texture; combining lacy torn edges with straight cut edges can look very effective. See chapter 3 for tips on tearing handmade paper.

Different ways to add texture – a checklist

If your design is looking a bit flat, add some texture to bring it to life. The following is a checklist of the different textures you can use:

- Textured paper or card, such as handmade, corrugated card or glitter card
- Textured sheet material, such as Angel Hair or Vivelle
- Sheets made from Angelina Fibres
- Loose glitter or glitter glue
- Flocking powder
- A strip of lace or ribbon
- Crumpled and sanded Core'dinations paper
- Dry embossed card
- Heat embossed card
- Liquid Appliqué
- Card glazed with UTEE or Glossy Accents
- Flower Soft or flock.

- Sakura Souffle or Glaze pens.

For a useful online demonstration of matting and layering, go to the video tutorials section of www.card-making-magic.com and click on 'Card making – matting and layering tutorial'.

More about choosing and combining colours

As already mentioned, it's often easier to choose your main embellishment or topper (the focal point of your card), and then pick your matting and layering colours to match.

As a starting point, use no more than three colours. If your topper has more than three colours (such as a multicoloured stamped image), pick the two or three most predominant colours for your matting and layering. This is not an unbreakable rule, but it's a useful guide to follow when you are starting out.

You also need to pick colours that work well together such as:

- The three primary colours, red, blue and yellow (a combination of two colours or all three together)
- Pink, lilac and violet (any two or all three)
- Turquoise, purple and emerald-green (any two or all three)
- Orange, red and yellow (any two or all three)
- Pale blue, silver, grey, white
- Cream, gold, red or blue
- Neutrals – beige, cream, ivory, taupe
- Earthtones – brown, terracotta, tan, yellow ochre, leaf-green, forest-green
- Black and white
- Pastels – pale pink, baby blue, lemon, pale green, light grey, pale purple
- Jewel colours – emerald-green, ruby-red, sapphire-blue, citrine yellow, amethyst purple, amber orange
- Green, red and gold or silver and purple for Christmas cards

- Pale green, pale pink and pale yellow for Easter cards

This list offers a few suggestions – but you do need to place your papers side by side to see how the shades work together. For example, pink can range from fuchsia (on the purple side of pink) to salmon (on the orange side of pink). Within a pink-dominated colour scheme, these two probably wouldn't work together – even though they are both called pink.

Having said which, rules in card making are there to be broken – and clashing colours might be just what you are looking for. Don't be afraid of colour. You're the designer, and playing around with different colours can throw up some unexpectedly successful combinations.

'Don't be afraid of colour. You're the designer, and playing around with different colours can throw up some unexpectedly successful combinations.'

Picking up colour accents

Choose card or paper that picks up the colour accent of a second paper. For example, you may have a floral patterned paper that is predominantly pink with green leaves. A plain green paper that matches the green of the leaves is guaranteed to go with the colours in the patterned paper.

Monochrome cards

Although the term monochrome is often used to describe cards with a black and white colour scheme, monochrome actually means a single colour.

Working with just one colour can be very effective, although it's not necessarily easier than combining two or three colours. Different shades of the same colour don't always go together – particularly blues, greens and greys. For example, an olive or khaki green doesn't work very well with a bright, emerald-green.

The other challenge of the monochrome card is finding ways to add visual interest. Combining different patterns can be quite difficult if they are in the same colour, and you also need to find ways of getting shapes to stand out. Texture (such as embossing) and embellishments (such as ribbons and jewels) are particularly important to the monochrome card.

Toppers and embellishments

Although matting and layering is important, the topper is the main event of your card and needs some careful thought. The following are just a few of the many available choices:

- A printed image from a craft CD or themed card-making kit
- A ready-printed, stamped or computer printed sentiment
- An outline sticker, backed with paper or coloured in
- A coloured or heat embossed stamped image
- A punched or die cut shape, embossed or decorated with ribbon, buttons, jewels, etc.
- Images cut from patterned scrapbook paper
- A decoupage, pyramage or invertage image
- A paper blossom or miniature bunch of flowers, tied with ribbon
- A bow with a dangly charm
- A single word made from coloured and patterned die cut letters

'Although matting and layering is important, the topper is the main event of your card.'

Always try out the embellishment against your matted and layered background, and see how it looks in different positions. Even though it is the focal point, it doesn't have to be right in the middle of the card. If you have covered your card with beautiful patterned and textured papers, placing your embellishment to one side can work well.

Odd numbers

You may choose to make up your embellishment from a group of small items, such as punched flowers, hearts or stars, a row of candles, die cut balloons or peel-off butterflies. An odd number tends to look the most pleasing – three flowers forming a triangle, five flags in a row, or three butterflies fluttering across the card front.

As always, this is not a hard and fast rule. Balanced rows of motifs in even numbers can look very effective, as can covering the card front with lots of shapes or using a carefully arranged jumble of motifs. As a starting point, however, sticking to the 3, 5, 7 rule is useful while you are building up your design skills.

Different arrangements

How you arrange your motifs can make a big difference to the appearance of the card. For example, taking just three butterflies as your main motif, there are numerous possibilities.

Your design decision will also be affected by how you make the butterflies (stamps, peel-offs, die cuts, punches, cut-out images), how you decorate them, whether they are all the same size or small, medium and large, whether they are identical or three different types, how you mat and layer, whether you add a sentiment, what other embellishments and finishing touches you decide to add . . . There's a lot to think about!

'How you arrange your motifs can make a big difference to the appearance of the card.'

Accents and finishing touches

When making a card, always keep in mind the 'less is more' rule. With so many fabulous bits and pieces to choose from, it's tempting to add just one more – until the card is overloaded and the design swamped. However, even when you have completed your matting and layering and stuck on your topper, the card may still need a little something else. This is where a small accent plays its part. The following is a reminder of the different embellishments that can be used to add that all-important finishing touch to your card:

- Flat-backed pearls
- Flat-backed jewels
- Small buttons
- A sprinkle of glitter
- Flower Soft
- A strip of ribbon or lace

- A bow
- Raffia or Baker's Twine.
- Glossy Accents
- Liquid Appliqué
- Brads
- A peel-off border strip

Choosing a style

The overall look, or style, of your card is yet another design decision to be made. Colours, patterns, textures and techniques all play their part in creating a particular style. When planning and designing a card, it's important to know what style you are aiming for, as this will affect your choice of papers, embellishments and techniques. There are many different design styles for card making. The following is just a small selection:

'Colours, patterns, textures and techniques all play their part in creating a particular style.'

Distressed

We have referred to the distressed style of crafting throughout this book. Also called vintage, weathered, grungy and shabby, distressed crafting uses techniques such as crumpling, sanding, fraying, tearing, inking around torn edges and covering images with a crackle glaze. Colours tend to be naturals and earth tones with vintage motifs such as ornate keys, clock faces, buttons, large blossoms, maps, scraps of old newsprint and cigarette card toppers. Tim Holtz is the king of distressed crafting and has a range of products designed to create a vintage look. For more information, see the book list and help list.

Rustic and homespun

Gingham, handmade paper, corrugated card, ribbon and buttons are suitable materials for the rustic and homespun style of crafting. Anything in natural colours works well for this style, as do organic materials such as raffia, hessian or twine. Typical motifs include leaves, shells, simple flower shapes and hearts, with gingham patterns in red or navy blue set alongside the neutral colours of speckled handmade paper or corrugated card. Think of simple country cottages with stripped wood furniture and corn dollies to get a feel for this style of card making.

Retro

'Retro' is short for 'retrospective'. In card making, retro can refer to any specific era such as the Victorian or Edwardian periods – although the term is most often used to describe the styles of the 1950s, 60s and 70s. If card making with a retro theme appeals, you can buy printed retro images and patterned papers with graphics that reflect the relevant era. Retro patterns from the second half of the 20th century tend to be made up of single colour areas (no shading or subtle patterning) and motifs such as circles, dots, slanted stripes and bold but simple flower shapes. Colours are typically brown teamed with lime green, pink or pale blue.

Cute

Cute cards usually feature a character. There are lots of cute characters to choose from – and they make a versatile and appealing theme to use in card making. Ranging from classic characters such as Forever Friends to cartoon ducks, elephants and children, the best sources for creating character images are clear or rubber stamps, craft CDs and ready-printed sheets. Crafter's Companion (www.crafterscompanion.co.uk) sells a wide range of character-based CDs, including Beatrix Potter, Flower Fairies and The Snowman. Another alternative is Joanna Sheen's House Mouse CD and stamp collection. The House Mouse series features a charming set of characters, specially designed for card making and with fewer copyright restrictions than the more familiar Crafter's Companion characters.

With such a wide variety to choose from, cute characters can be coloured, mounted and decorated in many different ways – particularly if you are stamping and colouring your own images. However, characters such as House Mouse, The Snowman, Forever Friends and Beatrix Potter work best with soft, pastel colours and pretty little details including bows, pearls and tiny flowers.

Copyright restrictions

If you want to sell cards that feature characters, check the manufacturer's Angel Policy or licensing agreement on their websites (see page 180 for more on Angel Policies and copyright).

Elegant

Elegant cards include elements such as flourishes, brocade embossed vellum, gold and silver foiled card, ribbons, bows and pearls. An elegant card might lean towards elegant and sophisticated with a colour scheme such as black, red and gold, or elegant and pretty with lacy punched borders and floral background papers. American designer Anna Griffin uses antique textiles and prints as the inspiration for her range of products. Dressed up with bows, lace and intricate die cut shapes, her floral motifs and papers are perfect for making cards that are both girly and elegant. For more about her range of products, visit www.annagriffin.com – and if you want to buy, www.qvcuk.com has one of the best selections in the UK.

Clean and clear-cut

The clean and clear-cut style could probably be described as the exact opposite of distressed crafting. Techniques such as dry embossing, with its sharp, crisp lines, simple punched borders and sentiments printed in a plain font are the hallmark of this style. Although attractive and eye-catching, the clean and clear-cut card has a minimalist feel. Edges are either straight or carefully shaped, colours are clear and images are arranged to create a neat, symmetrical look. Martha Stewart Crafts products are perfect for making this style of card, and the ideas on the Martha Stewart site give lots of suggestions and inspiration (www.marthastewart.com).

Finding inspiration

If you are stuck for card-making ideas, there are plenty of ways to find inspiration:

- Check the gallery sections of craft websites (see the help list).

- Search Pinterest for handmade cards (if you are interested in a particular technique, search for 'handmade cards' plus the name of the technique; for example, 'embossed handmade cards').
- Search YouTube for card-making demos and tutorials.
- Take inspiration from ready-made cards in shops.
- Watch Create and Craft TV (shopping channel).
- Check out card-making and paper craft magazines (see the help list).
- Borrow ideas for colour schemes, designs and motifs from wrapping paper, magazine pictures and handmade craft items.
- Join an online crafting forum (see the help list). Members often post photos of their creations, and are also happy to give design advice and ideas.
- Look out for local classes and card making groups.

Card making and the Internet

'Search YouTube for card making demos and tutorials.'

Throughout this book, we have referred to the Internet as a source of crafting materials, ideas and information. The Internet has had a huge influence on the development of card making as a hobby, with numerous online craft stores, blogs, forums and video tutorials. Even the largest and best-stocked craft shop can't sell anything like the choice of equipment and materials offered by the Internet – and, sadly, many craft shops have given up on the struggle to compete and closed down.

Not online?

It can be frustrating if you are not online, or unwilling to buy over the Internet. There are, however, many other sources of both card-making materials and information. Hobbycraft stores are still going strong and there should be at least some surviving craft shops in your area. A few online businesses will take orders by telephone and the TV shopping channels Create and Craft and QVC both offer a telephone ordering service (see the help list)

For inspiration and ideas, Create and Craft TV is a very useful source, and it's also worth looking out for local classes and card-making groups. To keep up to date with new developments, techniques and products, card-making magazines are indispensable – and they also include lots of card designs along with instructions (see the help list).

While there is no doubt that being online offers the card maker an immense number of possibilities, it is by no means essential if the Internet is not for you.

Selling your cards

Turning your hobby into a small business is a challenge, but immensely satisfying. Unless you are very focused and entrepreneurial, you are unlikely to earn much money. You can, however, make your hobby pay for itself – with the added thrill of knowing that someone likes your creation enough to buy it!

'Turning your hobby into a small business is a challenge, but immensely satisfying.'

If you want to try selling your cards, the following offers some tips and pointers:

Cello bags, labels and identification

Your cards will need protecting, and you also need to indicate the printed message inside and identify yourself as the maker:

Cello bags

These are clear bags that protect the card while enabling people to see the design. The cello surface can also be wiped clean with a damp cloth if you are selling your cards in a dusty environment. Cello bags are usually self-sealing, although some need to be sealed with a label.

Labels

Mini printed labels that state 'Happy Birthday' or 'This card has been left' blank are important for indicating the message inside. If your cello bag is not self-sealing, the label can double up as a seal.

Consider getting some 'not suitable for young children' labels to stick on the back of your cards – particularly if a card has small embellishments such as jewels or buttons. An 'inflammable' label should also be considered if you are using materials such as coloured foam sheets to make children's cards.

Identification

It's well worth including some way of identifying yourself on the back of each card. If you are taking your handmade card business seriously, you can print your details directly onto your card blanks. An easier option is to order bespoke printed labels with your business name and a website address or email. If you prefer to remain anonymous, leave out your contact details – but bear in mind that someone may want to get in touch to find out more about your work.

You can also get 'handmade by . . . ' clear or rubber stamps that you can stamp onto the back of the card and fill in with your name. This is a quick and easy option, although you need to use the technique with care to avoid it looking too amateurish. Pick coloured inks to fit in with the colour scheme of your card and practise your signature so that it looks attractive.

Sourcing cello bags and labels

www.pdacardandcraft.co.uk sells a wide range of cello bags and they also print white labels with your choice of message to stick onto the bag. www.able-labels.co.uk print attractive bespoke labels to go on the back of your cards – and you can choose from black, red or blue ink in three different fonts.

Designing cards to sell

Your reasons for selling your cards will influence the designs you come up with. If your main aim is to earn back some of the money you spend on your hobby, just carry on making the cards you love. If, however, you want to try setting up a serious business, you need to consider the following:

Design cards that are quick to make

Plan designs that can be made and reproduced quickly. It's quite challenging to come up with a simple card that is also eye-catching. Once you have some successful designs, look at how you can adapt them to make a range; for example, use the same motifs and card blank size, but arrange the motifs differently and use complementary colour schemes.

Prep your cards

Prepping (preparing) your cards is one of the keys to working quickly. If you plan to make a set of ten identical cards, prep all the sentiments together, punch and assemble all the flower embellishments in one go and so on. This is the most efficient way of working and it means you can speedily put together the actual cards.

'Once you have some successful designs, look at how you can adapt them to make a range.'

Watch your costs

Keep costs to a minimum. Realistically, it's hard to make a card for less than 30 or 40p, once you factor in the cost of the card blank, envelope, cello bag and labels. Some embellishments can work out quite expensive, and you also have to bear in mind adhesives, embossing powder and other consumables. Although you only use a tiny amount on each card, it all adds up. Costs involve some serious decisions. If you have set yourself a limit of 50p, and a special embellishment adds another 20p, does that embellishment make your card significantly more saleable? 20p may not sound like much, but the pennies quickly add up.

Ignore hourly rates of pay

However fast you manage to make and sell your cards, your actual hourly rate of pay will still be quite low. Don't work out what you are earning per hour as it can be too depressing! Concentrate instead on the fact that you are earning money by being creative and doing what you love.

Be ready for boredom

Be prepared for the tedium of repeating a design again and again. Make sure you give yourself time to develop new designs, both to keep your collection fresh and inject new enthusiasm into your project.

Outlets

Finding places to sell your cards is central to the success of your endeavours. Try the following:

Independent gift and craft shops and galleries

Take along your samples, choosing a quiet time so that the shop or gallery owner can have a proper look. Be prepared to accept sale or return, where the owner only pays you if a card is sold. In the current climate, shops and galleries are unlikely to buy your cards wholesale, however much they like them.

'People often remember that they need a card when they see one in an unexpected location.'

Local businesses

A friendly hairdresser, café, guest house or hotel can be a good outlet as you have no competition – and people often remember that they need a card when they see one in an unexpected location. Don't be afraid to ask – the worst that can happen is a refusal, and local businesses are often quite happy to pop a box of cards on their counter.

Workplaces

Ask friends and relatives if they will take a box of cards into their workplace. A large secondary school staffroom can be a particularly good place to sell, and you can offer to make a donation to the school, or give a batch of free cards for fundraising events. Provide an honesty box for the money and keep prices to the nearest pound or fifty pence to avoid complications with change. It's also worth providing a list with pen attached so that people can take a card, leave their name and pay later if they don't have the cash. If the workplace area is busy, ask your friend to check that your box doesn't end up pushed to the back of the table and out of sight.

Craft markets and school or church fetes

Card sellers have varying success at craft markets and school or church fetes. You need to sell enough cards to cover the cost of the stall – and you may need to wait for a slot in a craft market, as the organisers try to avoid having too many stalls with the same type of product. If you have a friend who also makes cards, or other craft items, it's worth sharing a stall. Selling card kits with a simple design and the materials to make the card can be very successful at school fetes – particularly if you aim the kits at children.

Car boot sales

As with markets, you need to cover the cost of your plot. People expect a bargain at a car boot sale, so you may find it hard to get a good price for handmade cards.

eBay

As with car boot sales, people look out for bargains on eBay. You may do better selling your own topper designs for other people to use in their card making. Have a look at the toppers that seem to be selling well on eBay before deciding whether to go down this route.

Online handmade craft stores

www.etsy.com is an American craft selling site, but it can be changed to a UK setting showing prices in pound sterling. www.folksy.com is similar to Etsy, but British based. In both cases, you set up your own virtual shop on the site to display your hand-crafted items. There are huge quantities of cards for sale on both sites, so you do need to offer something that stands out from the crowd. Reading the feedback for different sellers gives you a good idea of what sells well.

Selling through your own website

Setting up your own website to sell your cards is yet another option. If you decide to do this, you will need to research inexpensive ways of advertising the website – such as writing free pieces for article sites.

A card party

Selling cards at a card party gives you a captive market! Leading up to Christmas is a good time, but make sure you have lots of other special occasion cards for your guests to stock up on. For example, Valentine's Day is the first major card-giving occasion after Christmas. Set up facilities to make personalised Christmas cards at the party (ask someone to help with hosting duties to free you up) – or take orders if doing it on the spot is too tricky. Suggest to your guests that a selection of handmade cards makes a welcome present – particularly for an elderly person who can't get out very easily. You can also assemble packs of handmade notelets and tags to sell as gifts. If you have a crafting friend, join forces and host the party together.

> **Displaying your cards**
>
> You can put your cards in a box for people to rifle through – but a stand is much more eye-catching, and the cards are less likely to get damaged. www.stand-store.co.uk sells table-top cardboard stands that hold loads of cards. The stand is flat pack so it can easily be sent by post, and it's also straightforward to assemble. The white card surface is suitable for decorating if you want to personalise the stand.

'Selling cards at a card party gives you a captive market!'

Matching designs to outlets

Choose the right design and type of card for each outlet. For example, in a village craft shop with lots of pretty, chintzy items, a decorative floral card should sell well. In a high end urban gallery, something arty and cutting-edge might be more in-keeping with the style of the shop. If you are selling cards at a primary school fete, include lots of cards aimed at children's birthdays. If your local wholefood shop agrees to take some of your cards, go for a homespun style with recycled cardstock and natural embellishments.

Keep up with festivals and celebrations

Keep your outlets constantly stocked with a standard selection of birthday, anniversary, thank you, moving house, good luck, congratulations and all-purpose cards – but make sure you also follow the card-selling calendar. People are more likely to buy a special card for one-off events, and you need to make sure you have your supplies ready in good time. The major card-giving opportunities and events are as follows:

- Christmas (special cards for family members and close friends)
- Valentine's Day
- Chinese New Year
- Mother's Day
- Jewish Passover
- Easter
- Father's Day
- Summer weddings
- Good Luck (leading up to exams)
- Congratulations cards (following exams and graduation)
- Muslim Eid
- Hindu Diwali

Pricing

Pricing is tricky to get right. If you overprice, people won't buy. If you underprice, it can affect the customer's perception of your card as a quality item. You will also find that people vary as to what they are willing to spend on a card, handmade or otherwise. For example, you can charge higher prices in London than in the Midlands. You may find that it works to sell at different prices in different outlets. Having said that, try to ensure that outlets within an area are selling at the same price, as you don't want to upset anyone!

If you sell through a craft shop, they will probably price at double what you ask, and they may also add on VAT. For example, if you want to come away with £2 per card (£1.50 profit when you take into account your material costs), the shop will sell the card for at least £3.99. You need to work out whether this is a viable price for your card, or whether you should accept pocketing £1.50 or even £1 per card.

Discuss card prices with the shop owner as they know their market, and be prepared to adjust your expectations. Check out what handmade cards in your area sell for, and assess whether yours are similar in size, complexity and quality. Looking at the prices on the Folksy website can also give you some useful pointers.

The advantage of direct selling (in workplaces, card parties, markets or via your own website) is that you can pocket the entire selling price of the card – minus material costs and the rent for a stall. If people are willing to buy a handmade card, they are usually happy to pay at least £2 to £2.50 for something special and unique.

'Check your records regularly and work out which are your most popular designs.'

Keeping records and tax considerations

Prepare record sheets so you can make a note of every card you have made and every card you have sold. Check your records regularly and work out which are your most popular designs. Keep an eye on what type of card sells well – birthday, anniversary, all-purpose? Can you see a pattern of sales in your different outlets, and how could you respond to demand? For example, if all-purpose cards sell well in a particular school staffroom, start designing and making more so that you can give your customers a steady supply of new choices.

A list of the cards you are selling in each outlet is another important record. Give each card a code or name and make a duplicate list for you and the shop owner to sign and keep, as an agreed record of the stock they are holding. Hopefully, they themselves will keep records of what has been sold – but if they are not very organised, this record sheet can be invaluable in making sure you are paid correctly.

You also need to retain all your receipts and keep a record of the equipment and materials that you buy for card making. As a small business, you must have records for tax purposes, even if you do not earn up to the tax threshold. If you do have to pay tax on your card-selling income, the costs of your materials and equipment can be offset – hence the importance of keeping receipts and careful records. For more information about the tax implications of selling your cards, seek proper advice. As a starting point, visit www.hmrc.gov.uk.

Copyright and Angel Policies

If you intend to sell your cards, it is essential that you check the copyright or licensing agreement for the images, stamps, patterned papers, craft CDs and other materials you plan to use. In the crafting world, this is often called the Angel Policy.

'As a small business, you must have records for tax purposes, even if you do not earn up to the tax threshold.'

Some crafting companies have a generous, free-for-all policy; some place restrictions (such as not allowing you to sell more than 50 or 100 cards using a particular image); some allow you to sell at craft shows but not retail stores; some are only happy for you to sell cards using their images for charity – and some are not happy for you to sell at all. For example, the Disney Corporation are notoriously protective of their brand and will pursue anyone they discover using their images without permission.

Check a company's Angel Policy on their website – and if you can't find the details or are not sure exactly what the restrictions cover, email them and ask.

Summing Up

- Matting and layering provides a colourful, patterned background for your main embellishments. Matting and layering is a versatile technique and you can come up with endless ways of combining and arranging shapes, colour and patterns.
- Use no more than three different colours when you first start designing cards, and choose colours that work well together.
- Combine patterns with care, and bring a card to life by adding texture. Corrugated card, glitter, ribbon and embossing are just a few ways of introducing texture.
- Make sure you are happy with the positioning of your main embellishments before sticking them down, and add finishing touches such as glitter, flat-backed pearls, bows or border strips.
- Selling your cards on an ad hoc basis will enable you to recoup some of the cash you spend on your hobby. Turning card making into a serious business venture is much more challenging and will require you to design cards that can be made quickly.
- Do your homework and keep records so that you can work out which cards sell well, which outlets are the most profitable and whether you are selling at the right price. Records are also necessary for tax purposes, as selling your cards provides you with earned income.

Glossary

Acid free
The acid used in paper and card production causes damage to photographs. Acid-free products are safe to use with photographs – particularly important for scrapbooking.

Angel Hair
A sheet material that looks like flattened candyfloss.

Angel policy
A type of licence allowing you to use a card manufacturer's products when you make cards to sell. Some manufacturers give free usage whereas others allow only a certain number to be sold.

Anti-static bag
A powder-containing bag which reduces static build-up when rubbed over cardstock. Useful for projects involving glitter or embossing powder.

ATC
Short for Artist's Trading Card – a small hand-decorated card that is swapped amongst crafters to share techniques and ideas.

Blending tool
A handle with a felt pad attached, enabling the easy application and blending of inks, paints and other media.

Bone folder
A long, flat tool made of bone or plastic, used to press over the fold in a card to obtain a neat, sharp crease.

Brads
The crafting term for paper joiners. Brads consist of two flat pointed stems attached to a decorative head. To use, the stems are pushed through card and then split apart to fix the head to the other side of the card.

Brayer
A roller used for applying ink to a card surface. Brayering produces an extremely fine and even ink coverage.

Chipboard
A stiff recycled board that can be die cut and decorated.

Deckle edge
A deckle edge has a lightly torn effect. Card blanks can be bought with deckle edges and there are also fancy scissors and paper trimmers that produce deckle edging.

Decoupage
A paper crafting technique that involves building up an image in layers to give a three dimensional appearance.

Die cuts
Shapes made using a die cutting machine. They can either be purchased or you can make your own if you have a die cutting machine.

Digi-stamp
A black line image that can be downloaded from the Internet or a crafting CD and coloured in the same way as an image stamped with a rubber or clear stamp.

Distressed
A style of crafting that creates a weathered, aged, vintage look. Tim Holtz is one of the leading exponents of the distressed style.

Dome stickers
Rounded stickers made from clear, flexible epoxy resin that give a magnified look to whatever is beneath them.

Double-sided tape
Tape which is sticky on both sides. Useful for attaching flat embellishment such as card shapes or ribbon.

Eyelets
Small metal embellishments that create a lined hole when fixed onto a piece of card. A decorative way of creating a hole for ribbon, wire and so on.

Fancy scissors
Scissors with shaped blades, used to create decorative edges, including deckles, scallops and zigzags.

Fixative
A spray that is used to fix powdery media, such as chalk, to a surface, and prevent it from smudging.

Foam pads
Small pads of foam that are sticky on both sides. Used to give an embellishment or topper a raised look when attached to the card blank.

Font
The style and size of a letter.

Grungeboard
Designed by Tim Holtz, Grungeboard shares some similarities with chipboard, but it is flexible and will not tear. It will also take any amount of liquid decoration as it is not porous like chipboard.

Grunge
Another term for the 'distressed' style of crafting.

GSM
Stands for grams per square metre – a way of measuring paper weight. The higher the number, the heavier the paper.

Guillotine
A paper cutter with a handle blade attached to a base. The blade is pulled down to make a straight cut in a piece of paper of card.

Heat gun
An electrically operated tool that produces a gentle current of hot air – not unlike a hairdryer, but much hotter. Used for heat embossing, shrink plastic and speeding up the drying time for wet media such as pigment inks.

Invertage
A paper craft technique similar to pyramage, except that the layers create depth rather than height. The frames left over from cutting out shapes to make pyramage can be used for invertage.

Iris folding
A paper craft technique where folded strips of coloured paper are taped behind a shaped aperture to create a design.

Light box
An opaque white plastic box containing a light bulb and used as a work surface for dry embossing.

Lignin free
Lignin is a substance in wood that is also present in paper. Over time, it discolours the paper and damages photos. Along with acid-free products, lignin-free card and paper should be used for paper craft projects that are made to be kept long term.

Low-tack tape
Used to temporarily fix items such as stencils to card, as it can be removed without tearing the card.

Matting and layering
Building up layers of shapes (mats) in different patterns, colours and textures to create an interesting background for the focal point of your card.

Medallions
Ornate decorative motifs, usually based on a circular shape. Medallions usually come in different sizes so they can be layered, and they can be made using specially designed stamps, peel-offs or dies.

Melting pot
A heat-resistant pot that is used to melt crafting media such as thick embossing powder or wax.

Mica powders
Coloured pigment powders containing tiny flecks of mica to add shimmer. The powders can be mixed with water and used as paints or added to other media such as clear embossing powder.

Mirri card
Card with a highly reflective surface. Gold and silver mirri card are the most common, although it can be obtained in other colours and also as a paper.

Monochrome
Describes a project that uses shades of just one colour. The term is often used to describe black and white cards.

Mulberry paper
A thin handmade paper made from mulberry fibres, with a characteristically soft, feathery texture.

Nesting punches and dies
Punches or dies for die cutting machines that consist of the same shape but in a series of sizes. The punched or die cut shapes can be layered to give a three-dimensional look.

Outline peel-off stickers
Stickers consisting of just the outlines of an image, as if it has been drawn with a thick pen.

Peel-offs
Another term for stickers.

Pergamano
The brand name for the tools used in parchment craft. Nowadays, the term is often used to describe the craft itself.

Pokey tool
A tool with a sharp metal point, used for piercing holes, removing peel-offs from sheets and many other tasks and techniques.

PVA glue
White, all-purpose glue that is safe for children to use. Dries clear but is not waterproof. The tacky or hi-tack version in gold bottles is much more suitable for sticking heavy embellishments.

Pyramage
A form of decoupage that involves building up a series of picture details to create a pyramid shape.

Scalloped edge
An edge with a wavy pattern. Card blanks can be bought with a scalloped edge, or created using fancy scissors, a border punch or a paper trimmer with a scalloped blade.

Scrapbooking
An American paper craft that involves mounting photographs on a page and decorating with matting and layering, embellishments and sentiments. Many card making and scrapbooking techniques overlap.

Shrink plastic
A special kind of plastic that reduces in size when heated. It can be stamped on and then made smaller with a heat gun to create a miniature embellishment.

Silicone glue
A clear waterproof glue that keeps its shape when dry, making it useful for decoupage and creating other three dimensional effects. Not suitable for children to use.

Tape runners
A small, hand-held device that leaves a strip of dry adhesive when rolled over paper or card. Tape runners come in both disposable and refillable versions.

Teabag folding
Teabag folding is a paper folding technique that can be used to make intricate embellishments for cards. It is said to have originated from folding the decorative envelopes used to hold teabags – hence the name.

Template
A template is a shape that can be drawn around.

Toppers
A topper is a focal point decoration for a card. The term is often used for ready-made matted and layered embellishments that can be stuck straight onto the card front, without any further embellishment.

UTEE
Stands for Ultra Thick Embossing Enamel. UTEE is a coarse thermographic powder that melts when heated to form a thick enamelled layer.

Vellum
A translucent paper, similar in texture to tracing paper. It is available in a range of different colours and is good for tearing and dry embossing.

Help List

Crafting advice, tutorials and cards to make

www.allcrafts.net

Lots of free crafting patterns including envelope templates.

www.card-making-magic.com

A site with some great video tutorials on different aspects of card making.

www.copicmarker.com

Lots of fascinating tips and tutorials from the Copic Marker home site.

www.craftsbycarolyn.co.uk

A great range of tips and how-to articles, plus an active forum where you can chat about card making and ask for advice.

Create and Craft TV

www.createandcraft.tv
A TV shopping channel dedicated to craft and card making. Lots of great demos from some of the top names in UK crafting – including Joanna Sheen, Barbara Gray, Dawn Bibby, Leonie Pujol, Stephanie Weightman and Sheena Douglass.

www.fredaldous.co.uk

This site has a great selection of gems in different sizes and colours. Although they are not the cheapest option, they are superb quality and you can also choose the exact colours that you want.

www.fiskarscraft.co.uk

Home site for Fiskars, the orange-handled scissors company. Lists all their products and lots of card-making ideas.

www.handmade-craft-ideas.com

Covers various crafts, with a particularly good section on paper quilling.

www.handyhippo.co.uk

Online craft store with useful articles, tips and card projects.

www.joannasheen.co.uk

Useful articles on different aspects of card making and lots of card ideas with instructions – plus a friendly and well-moderated forum.

www.marthastewart.com

Some great projects using Martha Stewart Crafts' products to create cards in Martha Stewart's distinctive style.

www.pinterest.com

Pinterest has a huge gallery of card samples. Search the site for a particular topic, such as handmade embossed cards.

www.promarker.info

Lots of advice and tips for using ProMarker pens, plus a gallery of samples.

www.rangerink.com

Another destination for the distressed crafter. Ranger make the Tim Holtz collection and this site has great product descriptions, as well as lots of tips and techniques, video tutorials and projects.

www.sakuraofamerica.com

Information about the Sakura Gelly Roll gel pens, plus some fabulous ideas for using them.

www.thecraftbarn.co.uk

Website with information on various topics – plus crafting classes and demos for those in the Surrey area.

www.timholtz.com

For devotees of the distressed style of crafting, Tim Holtz's site is a must. It includes product lists, lots of video tutorials and a blog with some great links.

www.tsukineko.com

Good tips and techniques for using the Tsukineko range of ink and glue pads – including StazOn, VersaMark, VersaMagic and The Essential Glue Pad.

www.youtube.com

Huge selection of video tutorials. Search for a specific crafting technique and, in most cases, you will be spoilt for choice.

Online craft stores

www.annagriffin.com

Beautiful floral themed products, inspired by vintage textiles. This is an American site – to buy within the UK, see QVC overleaf.

www.bazzillbasics.com

Although you can't buy from this site, it lists every sheet of Bazzill's Basics cardstock, along with photos and a blog.

www.claritystamp.co.uk

Excellent quality clear stamps and accessories. Includes the Clarity Club with step-by-step stamping projects and free stamps.

www.craftcds.co.uk

A huge selection of crafting CDs from different designers.

www.craftcreations.com

Excellent online craft store, with an outstanding collection of card and paper – particularly handmade paper. Also, a great choice of own brand peel-off stickers.

www.crafterscompanion.co.uk

Good source of embossing boards and character CDs and kits, including The World of Beatrix Potter.

www.craftisland.co.uk

Fabulous selection of buttons, including different colours, sizes, shapes and patterns.

www.craftsuprint.com

A huge range of card-making downloads.

www.craftsuperstore.co.uk

A site that stocks a great range of well-known crafting names, including Martha Stewart Crafts' distinctive punches and glitters and Tim Holtz Distress crafting range.

www.fantasticribbons.com

Ribbon in just about every colour, width, pattern and finish imaginable.

www.flower-soft.co.uk

Site selling Flower Soft and related products.

www.freecraftdownloads.co.uk

Free printable images for decoupage, pyramage and invertage. Also, tags, toppers, characters and digi stamps.

www.hobbycraft.co.uk

Website for the well-known craft retail company, including a store locator if you want to shop in store rather than online.

www.pdacardandcraft.co.uk

Great range of card blanks, envelopes, inserts and cello bags. You can choose the colour, size, cardstock and quantity you want and the website also tells you which envelopes, inserts and cello bags you need for each size card blank. Good value and excellent customer support.

www.perfectparchmentcraft.com

A site dedicated to tools and accessories for Pergamano parchment craft.

www.pinflair.co.uk

Home of the much-loved Pinflair Glue Gel, amongst many other useful products.

www.qvcuk.com

One of the best UK outlets for American designer Anna Griffin's floral themed products.

www.rainbowsilks.co.uk

Sells all the equipment needed for using Angelina Fibres.

www.theglittergirls.co.uk

Wide selection of embossing boards – the Glitter Girls' speciality (catch their demos on Create and Craft TV).

www.woodware.co.uk

The general public can't purchase from this site, but it lists and illustrates every craft punch in the huge Woodware collection, plus stockists.

www.3dsheets.com

Decoupage sheets with unusually good-quality graphics for a free download.

Specialist equipment

www.anythingleft-handed.co.uk

A site selling left-handed scissors.

www.peta-uk.com

Good range of ergonomically designed scissors for people with arthritis and other dexterity problems.

Card making and crafting magazines

Card making & Papercraft

Quick Cards Made Easy
Craftseller
www.cardmakingandpapercraft.com

Crafts Beautiful Magazine

www.crafts-beautiful.com

Let's Make Cards

www.letsmakecards.com

Making Cards

www.makingcardsmagazine.com

PaperCrafter Magazine

www.papercraftermagazine.co.uk

Parchment Craft

www.parchmentcraftmagazine.com

Simply Cards & Papercraft

Papercraft Essentials
Creative Stamping
Creative Card making
Complete Card making
Scrapbook magazine
www.practicalpublishing.co.uk

Book List

A Compendium of Curiosities Tim Holtz, Advantus Corp (Jacksonville, Florida) 2010: £16.74

Artist Trading Cards (Twenty to Make) Leonie Pujol, Search Press Ltd (Tunbridge Wells, Kent) 2007: £4.99

Between the Sheets with Angelina: A Workbook for Fusible Fibres Alysn Midgelow-Marsden, Word4Word (Evesham, Hereford and Worcester), 2003, £9.95

Cards for Men & Boys: Over 70 Inspirational Designs for the Men in Your Life Elizabeth Moad, David and Charles (Newton Abbot, Devon) 2006: £12.99

How to Scrapbook Joy Aitman and Sarah McKenna, Search Press Ltd (Tunbridge Wells, Kent) 2006: £10.99

Iris Folding (Passion for Paper) Michelle Powell, Search Press Ltd (Tunbridge Wells, Kent) 2008: £9.99

Joanna Sheen's World of Cards Joanna Sheen, Search Press Ltd (Tunbridge Wells, Kent) 2009: £18.99

Just the Right Words: Over 400 Messages and Motifs for Cardmakers and Crafters Judith Wibberley, David and Charles (Newton Abbot, Devon) 2007: £9.99

Paper Bouquet: Using Paper Punches to Create Beautiful Flowers Susan Tierney Cockburn, Lark Books (Asheville, North Carolina) 2008: £8.99

Paper Punching (Passion for Paper) Michelle Powell, Search Press Ltd (Tunbridge Wells, Kent) 2007: £9.99

Parchment Craft Carla Larter, Crowood Press Ltd (Marlborough, Wiltshire) 2008: £9.99

Punch Your Art Out Vol 2 Memory Makers, (F& W Media, New York) 2002, £9.99

Quick and Clever Handmade Cards: Over 80 Projects and Ideas for All Occasions Julie Hickey, David and Charles (Newton Abbot, Devon) 2004: £12.99

Quilling: Techniques and Inspiration Jane Jenkins, Search Press Ltd (Tunbridge Wells, Kent) 2003: £8.99

Simply Sensational Rubber Stamping Jane Pinder, David and Charles (Newton Abbot, Devon) 2006: £12.99